Wellbeing

THE ART OF LIVING SERIES
Series Editor: Mark Vernon

From Plato to Bertrand Russell philosophers have engaged wide audiences on matters of life and death. *The Art of Living* series aims to open up philosophy's riches to a wider public once again. Taking its lead from the concerns of the ancient Greek philosophers, the series asks the question "How should we live?". Authors draw on their own personal reflections to write philosophy that seeks to enrich, stimulate and challenge the reader's thoughts about their own life. In a world where people are searching for new insights and sources of meaning, *The Art of Living* series showcases the value of philosophy and reveals it as a great untapped resource for our age.

Published
Clothes   *John Harvey*
Deception   *Ziyad Marar*
Fame   *Mark Rowlands*
Hunger   *Raymond Tallis*
Illness   *Havi Carel*
Pets   *Erica Fudge*
Sport   *Colin McGinn*
Wellbeing   *Mark Vernon*
Work   *Lars Svendsen*

Forthcoming
Death   *Todd May*
Middle Age   *Chris Hamilton*
Sex   *Seiriol Morgan*

Wellbeing

Mark Vernon

ACUMEN

To Guy Reid and Andrew Day, for the wellbeing
they have taught and brought.

First published in 2008 by Acumen

Acumen Publishing Limited
Stocksfield Hall
Stocksfield
NE43 7TN
www.acumenpublishing.co.uk

ISBN: 978-1-84465-153-5

British Library Cataloguing-in-Publication Data
A catalogue record for this book is available
from the British Library.

Designed and typeset by Kate Williams, Swansea.
Printed and bound by Biddles Ltd, King's Lynn.

Contents

Acknowledgements

My very great thanks go to Steven Gerrard at Acumen, for commissioning both *Wellbeing* and *The Art of Living* series. I must also express my deep appreciation to Richard Schoch, David Cooper, Chris Hamilton and Jean Kazez who read earlier drafts and offered very helpful critiques, and to Richard Kraut for his words on the shape and content of the book. Thanks too to Kate Williams for expert copy-editing.

Introduction: happy yet?

If you were a pollster and asked me on the street, clipboard in hand, whether or not I was happy I would probably reply in the positive, "Yes", with a firm tone. If you pressed me and asked me to place my happiness on a scale of 1 to 5, I'd pause for a moment and position myself, say, as a 4 – perhaps 4 to 5 if the sun were shining.

If you were a politician, party badge on your lapel, and asked me the same question on the street I would probably reply more equivocally. You'd get a "Yes, but …", the "but" being my opportunity to express anxieties about foreign wars, global warming or "selfish capitalism", as clinical psychologist Oliver James has called it. I'd give the impression that personally I am happy, more or less. But I think there are some pretty unhappy-making events and forces in the world around us. In my pessimistic moments I might even say they are out of control. I'd be happier with a visionary leader who I felt could address them.

If you were a psychologist and asked me in the lab whether I was happy I'd have a different reply again. Now I'd be feeling that much of the time I am pretty fulfilled. I am passionate about my work, blessed in my relationships, engaged by my interests and more or less content with my lot. OK, so I do have some sleepless nights troubled by work. Well, in fact, probably at least one a week. And I can worry quite irrationally about how I would cope if my partner died and, sentimental as it is to admit it, I know I'd be seriously upset if my cat passed away, although I'd cope. (Of course, I shouldn't say "if" my cat passed away, for my cat will die,

1

but isn't everyone allowed a little denial about mortality, doctor?) Also, there is that discontented side to me that, say, would like it if we had a second home in Kent – nothing extravagant – and more cash to regularly escape the city. But, hey, most of the time these concerns are background. They've only overcome me two or three times in my life when subterranean bleakness has been unleashed and I've become depressed.

If you were a philosopher and wrote a book asking whether I was happy ... then you'd be talking! I'd argue that the problem with happiness is that there's a Catch-22 implicit in the pursuit of it. With a little thought I'd come up with some metaphors to capture the enigma. For example, think of the situation of the "resting" actor who can only find work it they have an agent, but can only find an agent if they have work. Or do you remember random-dot stereograms, those fuzzy optical illusions that require you to look through them to catch sight of the three-dimensional image in them? Trying to see the pictures in them is like the pursuit of happiness in as much as the picture seems to dematerialize if it comes too much into focus. Maybe the search for happiness is a bit like the quest for God. All the greatest mystics testify that there is something profoundly paradoxical about divinity: God is bliss to know but is known as unknowable. Augustine fell back to asking, "What do I love when I love God?" Replace "God" with "happiness" and doesn't the new question also make sense?

Perhaps our conversation would continue. We'd ask a different question: not "Are you happy?", but "What do you think it takes to be happy?" Here I could be clearer. I'd say that I suspect my own happiness is not actually best served by focusing my efforts on my own happiness. That sounds contradictory. And yet when I think about it, my intuition is that the sources, even the possibility, of happiness are located in something other than essentially self-centred concerns. To put it another way, it is futile to think of life mostly as a fight for felicity, although often, if I am honest, I act as if it were.

This essay is part of my own work in progress, like life. But it is born out of my struggle to see, as clearly as I can, just where or what that joy-giving something else might be. I want to push as deeply as I can into the question of human wellbeing: to look beneath the surface happiness represented by the approach of the pollster and understand more about the uncertainties that the questions of a psychologist or philosopher would throw up. They may be uncertainties, often well buried. But they are also opportunities, to not just have a life but to know life in all its fullness.

Which is to say that happiness – or wellbeing, my preferred word because I believe it carries wider, deeper connotations – is an excellent and essential matter to consider, even for the more or less happy. In large part, philosophy and religion both owe their existence to the fact that it is hard to get wellbeing right, or the fear that it may entirely pass us by. Who would want to die with the lingering suspicion that they'd lived but perhaps not as well as they might? The greatest thinkers on happiness have talked around their subject. They are like fine novelists probing human character by sly insights not crude caricature. Aristotle's word for happiness was *eudaimonia*, assuming for the moment that its meaning is something close to our own. It is a compound word: *eu* means good; *daimon* means daemon or spirit – entities that mediate between the everyday world and the world of the gods. *Eudaimonia* could be crudely translated as "well-godedness" or "a good god within". Understanding what that might mean will be a key part of this discussion.

That happiness cannot be attained by straightforwardly making it a goal in life was also picked up by the secular nineteenth-century British philosopher John Stuart Mill (1989: ch. 5). He argued that the trick is to discover what you can wholeheartedly pursue that would incidentally bring happiness in its wake. It is a by-product, he concluded. But disinterestedness in your own happiness is hard to pull off: "Ask yourself whether you are happy, and you cease to be so", he warned. The impasse would be like that of a young artist who becomes obsessed with whether they will be great. What they need to do is shake that off and become obsessed, say, with light, London smog and lilies, like Claude Monet: it is only such passion that might make their work, as a by-product, momentous. That's another facet to consider.

Or maybe the problem is that happiness is what might be called the "secret motive" of our actions: secret not just because it often lies behind what we decide to do in life, but also because it is generally pretty unclear to most of us how those actions might actually produce the happiness we hope to win. We live thinking that they might yield contentment, rather than with a sure conviction that they will. Isn't it true that many people spend much of their lives pouring energy into pursuits that they presume will lead to an abundance of joy only to become casualties of the consumer age – burnt out, drugged up or in debt? The American writer Nathaniel Hawthorne is one of many fiction writers to capture the crux of the matter: "Happiness is a butterfly, which, when pursued, is always beyond our grasp, but which, if you will sit down quietly, may alight upon you", he wrote. It sounds beautiful, until you ask yourself how frequently butterflies actually settle on a human perch. I've never seen it myself.

This is the side of happiness that makes its pursuit a worry; most long for it, but maybe the truth is that it comes permanently only to a few – the rich, the fulfilled, the lucky. Pondering what might maximize their chances of enjoying its light led the Stoics to conclude that if you are serious about happiness you must be prepared to face some fierce demands. For them, the happy-seeking individual must strive to rise above his or her petty concerns, comprehend the ways of nature and change their life to live in accordance with her universal rules and currents. The Stoic Marcus Aurelius was also the Roman Emperor. He thought happiness could belong to you but only if you could "leave everything past behind you, entrust the future to providence, and if you arrange the present in accordance with piety and justice" (*Meditations*, Book 12). Needless to say, a reorientation of the fears and concerns that crowd in to fill most people's lives is far easier said than done. It requires a massive change of consciousness. To illustrate the extent of the challenge, the original Stoics of ancient Athens used to say that you had to change your outlook on life so radically that, hand on heart, you could call yourself happy if you owned nothing, were hated by everyone and found yourself strapped to the rack. Only a wise person could have such moral fortitude, they concluded, and they are as rare a creature as the phoenix. Happiness is a jewel. Ideally it is shown off in the beautiful setting of a rich human life. But it should shine through even if the individual should fall on hard times and into the gutter.

Questions then. Is happiness the by-product of a life or can it be found directly, in anything from family and friends, to fudge cake and a cappuccino? Does it have resilient qualities or is it more a matter of happenstance? Is its pursuit as taxing as ascending Everest or as easy as coming home? Little wonder that the subject fills the shelves of bookshops and attracts such lively debate. That is surely a product of these tensions.

The tougher conceptions of contentment are unsettling, although I must confess a fascination with them too, for the very reason that they present a challenge; if wellbeing is worth having, as it is, but is not immediately obvious, then perhaps this elusiveness is to be expected, as an expression of life's weight and value. This would then be related to something else that I feel about much popular advice on happiness: that it can sound like so much motherhood and apple pie – "work less", "maintain families", "earn enough", "keep fit", "find meaning", "enjoy freedoms". If it is as straightforward as that, I want to ask, then why do we not just get on and do it? If a good life were that transparent then we would follow the formula and the self-help industry would effectively cease, which it clearly has not.

Higher flourishing

The problem, and the reason why self-help doesn't really satisfy, stems from the idea of happiness that lies behind it. It is a notion that is dominant in the West. In fact, it is so omnipresent that it is hard to think about happiness, let alone wellbeing, unless it has been talked through, and, in many ways, talked out. Moreover, this dominant idea of happiness fails, I think, to pinpoint the fundamental issue for human wellbeing today. This is not so much about having a good life, which makes it sound little harder than finding a decent golf club or choosing whether to wear a jacket or jumper to keep out the cold. It is about the search for the good in life. It is this latter matter, I believe, that is so crucial for us today.

What I mean can be seen by reflecting on nearly all the older philosophical and religious traditions. They argue, in one way or another, that wellbeing happens at two levels. The first might be called "lower flourishing", borrowing an expression from the philosopher Charles Taylor (2007). Lower flourishing is thriving in the everyday. It is having good friends, a happy family, fulfilling employment, pleasurable leisure. They are elements that contribute to different parts of normal human existence. Working on these separate parts with the aim of building a steady portfolio of satisfactions, is what contemporary happiness movements encourage us to do. In the modern world, there is every opportunity to be at least good enough at many of them. And if life should throw things up that are more difficult to cope with, we have reason to guide us through and, as a safety-net, health care. These things are all good.

But lower flourishing used to be only half the story. The second level is what Taylor calls "higher flourishing". It is concerned with the larger perspective on life. It is prior to lower flourishing because it informs and shapes the humdrum. It provides a sense of intrinsic meaning or overall direction or deeper purpose. It originates not in daily activities but in ethics, spirituality or religion. It is not just a concern with the piecemeal constituents of a good life, but a love of the good itself and a search for that good in life. It is an attention to what most fundamentally matters, perhaps even more than family and friends, although actually I think the search makes them matter all the more. It would also not decry fudge cake and cappuccino, at least on occasion. It is characterized as a transcendent commitment that if not imagined as belonging to another world is felt as a pull towards something that is deeper than or beyond the concerns that an individual would otherwise have for himself or herself. Like Nelson Mandela, whom crowds flock just to glimpse, or religious saints, whom our ancestors gathered to worship, higher flourishing has the magnetic allure of what is good in itself. It is about the spirit level.

The notion that higher flourishing was a fundamental step in cultivating wellbeing went almost without question until modern times. An ancient philosopher's days, for example, were more like those of a holy monk than a contemporary academic. Aristotle, for one, argued that the well-lived life consists of whatever cultivates a growing appreciation of divine truth: in the *Eudemian Ethics*, he wrote that the best action is "whatever choice or possession of natural goods – bodily goods, wealth, friends and the like – will most conduce to the contemplation of God" (8.1259b). The individual's relationship to the transcendent was key. As he wrote in the *Nicomachean Ethics*:

> We must not heed those who advise us to think as human beings since we are human and to think mortal things since we are mortal, but we must be like immortals insofar as possible and do everything toward living in accordance with the best thing in us.   (10.1177B33

It was not only the heights of pleasure or even the lengths of meaning that mattered; fundamentally, it was the depths of that

which is ultimately beyond us, mentally, morally and metaphysically. A desire for these mysteries was central to a life that could
robustly be said to be going well. Why? In short, because mentally,
morally and metaphysically, human beings are limited; we are, it
might be said, "vertically challenged". But, and this is the source
of hope, it is possible to be keenly conscious of that fact: worries
about happiness might actually be a first, necessary step. Thus,
the belief was that although the source of human wellbeing is ultimately beyond human comprehension, it is only ultimately beyond
human comprehension, to borrow a distinction made by literary
critic George Steiner. Before the ultimate – "before" in the sense of
both "before we are there" and "standing before this amazing sight"
– there could be faith that higher flourishing is possible because
the best in humankind is godlike. Being "like immortals insofar as
possible" responds to that.

A similar concern echoed across other ancient schools of
thought. For the Stoics, happiness rested on submitting to nature,
which taken as a whole was divine. For Christian writers such as
Augustine and Aquinas, wellbeing was found in the love of God.
For Eastern thinkers such as the Buddha, it emerged as the illusions
of the ego crumbled in the transcendence of enlightenment. Even
for schools such as the Epicureans, who argued that no one need
fear the gods because they cannot touch you, the goal of life was a
tranquil, blissful state that imitated the life of Olympus.

Transcendent troubles

What we make of the transcendent – whether we can any longer have
faith in it – is, I believe, the crunch issue for contemporary wellbeing.
I'd go so far as to say that on it rests the success of all other attempts to
live life well. The transcendent is "a root-impulse of the human spirit
to explore possibilities of meaning and of truth that lie outside of

empirical seizure or proof", as Steiner put it in *Real Presences* (1989: 225). That attitude could be called religious in a diffuse sense: it has a "sense and taste for the infinite", to use the phrase of the theologian Friedrich Schleiermacher (1988: 103). Where it differs from religion – if you'll allow me to attempt a subtle but necessary differentiation of terms – is that this feeling for transcendence does not automatically necessitate belief in God. It is also for this reason that the transcendent is sometimes referred to as the transcendental, in part to distinguish it from any explicit belief in God. It does imply an intuition that there is a spiritual existence beyond the empirical world of the senses that is nonetheless connected to it. In this sense it is other-worldly, although other-worldliness can be misleading since the point about the transcendent is not that it is "elsewhere"; it is here. The transcendent is that which deepens the sense of humdrum reality, as opposed to suggesting a reality in which this world matters not at all. It is the reason for higher flourishing.

Personally, I write as an agnostic and so, here, will not make any suppositions about the existence, or not, of a realm inhabited by the divine: transcendence is meant in the sense of the transcendental. That said, we must not flinch before it and, I hope to persuade you, must wager on it, again to echo Steiner. For it is highly problematic in modern times, and I don't just mean for those who won't, don't or can't do religion. Frequently, the transcendent is made an optional extra for the theologically inclined, a sort of spiritual plug-in; at worst, it is discarded with force. To the secular mind it can appear elitist, irrational or superstitious. Many atheists would argue that to think in this way is to indulge the habits of an enchanted yesteryear. Today, they say, we must grow up and be prepared to face the possibility that there is no overarching purpose in life, or at least if there is to be one, we have to create it for ourselves.

However, the challenge of the transcendent persists. It lies, I would argue, at the heart of the contemporary interest in and, more precisely, the contemporary anxiety about happiness. I suspect it is a big part of why the ancient ideas about the good life seem so challenging and many of the modern prescriptions so ephemeral. To put it another way, it is the people who are most unsure about the quality of their happiness who enquire most insistently about it. Don't folk ask whether you are enjoying yourself only when you aren't? Isn't this what we are questioning today, in movements from New Age to positive psychology?

The structure of the book is roughly this. First, in Chapters 1 and 2, I'll try to unpick the reasons for the crisis about happiness. In Chapter 1, I'll turn to the most common understanding of happiness, that of happiness as pleasure or positive emotion. It is too weak for a number of reasons. For instance, if you take your happiness to be more or less identical with your pleasures, be they refined or coarse, then, like pleasure, it will rise and fall like the tides, although without the predictably: a source of anxiety at least as much as contentment. Worse, the pleasures we seek are not always the pleasures we find, which is why pleasure-seeking is a pretty sure route to its opposite, pain. This is the second subject in Chapter 1, for, in fact, suffering plays a crucial part in wellbeing, difficult as it may be to say so.

That makes sense when wellbeing is considered in the context of the subject for Chapter 2, which is meaning. As I see it, this is the sticking point for us human beings: we are creatures who, in the last analysis, seek meaning. The Russian novelist Vladimir Nabokov thought the difference between people and other animals hung on this:

Being aware of being aware of being. In other words, if I not only know that I am but also know that I know it, then I belong to the human species. All the rest follows: the glory of thought, poetry, a vision of the universe. In that respect, the gap between ape and man is immeasurably greater than the one between amoeba and ape.   (1969)

Considering what makes for meaning, and how widely it differs from happiness based on pleasure, leads me to a suggestion about the quest for wellbeing. In line with the indirect nature of happiness, I think it might be good for our happiness if, at this particular juncture, we actually stopped talking about our happiness – talk that seems so caught up in the impossible quest for sustainable pleasures – and switched instead to the notion of wellbeing (hence too the title of the book). Wellbeing might allow us to reintegrate into our quest some of the concerns that the ancient philosophers saw as so central.

This leads into Chapter 3 because the most important of these concerns stems from a further reflection about what makes life meaningful for human beings. It is not in our nature to seek just any meaning, I believe. We seek meaning in that which lies above, through or outside the common-or-garden. In this, we are again quite different from other animals. If they have no inclination to understand themselves, not being aware of being aware of being, they most certainly do not seek to do so by placing themselves within a frame of being whose boundaries they cannot see. They are happy with life, or not, as it mundanely comes to them. When did a dog, cat, dolphin, monkey or ape ask why there is something rather than nothing? Or perhaps think on this: dogs, cats, dolphins, monkeys and apes have variously been treated as gods by human beings, or at least as tokens of a higher reality, but we can be quite sure that statues or mummies or paintings of human beings have never been as gods to them, even when we have lauded it over them as keepers and masters. In Chapter 3, I shall explore what the transcendent variously means to us today, living in a world that has forgotten many of the skills of higher flourishing. Although it turns out that even if we have forgotten some skills, we have not, I think, forgotten the lure of the transcendent. It is, in fact, all around.

From that emerges another point, the central issue in Chapter 4. There is, I think, a kind of minimal requirement to satisfy the transcendent demands of human wellbeing: what is meaningful must be conceived of as good but ultimately inexpressible. That might seem like another paradox or self-contradiction. It certainly pushes us to the limits of language. (In this chapter I shall consider some of the objections that can be made against such a conception of the transcendent too.) And yet without that ineffable quality there is too great a risk that meaning collapses back on to the all too human and unravels in our hands. This, in turn, means that there is an irreducibly intuitive component to the pursuit of the good in life: it will involve rational argument, personal advice and political debate, but more fundamentally can be thought of as a kind of spiritual exercise that awakens the individual to, and orientates them towards, the good – which, in turn, draws them body, mind and spirit.

To put it another way, if our wellbeing depends in some way on that which is beyond us – or at the very least draws us to a state of purpose or serenity as if from outside – it is by definition in large part unfamiliar, unusual and unknown. It emerges as something shown or revealed, not told or made. It is an experience not a rule; although informed by reason it outstrips rationality. This is what we shall come to in Chapter 5. Theologians would call it a mystery of infinite worth. Philosophers might say it was an unconditional moral demand. Plato proposed a synthesis of these two, imagining how love can lead us to wellbeing. And love is the main focus of the last chapter.

Plato thought that the basic question to ask if you are serious about life is not "What will you do?", "How will you live?" or even "Are you a good or bad person?", although you will ask all these things. It was this: what do you love? The point is that we become what we love, or at least strive to draw close to it. Further, we can only understand that which we love – understand in the subjective sense of being acquainted with it – by knowing it from within. "The quality of our attachments is the quality of our understanding", wrote Iris Murdoch (1992: 295). Gaining such insight has much to do with our being: who we are as individuals and as people. When we are talking about the good in life, that concerns what we morally make of ourselves. "Knowledge we could never attain, remaining what we are, may be attainable in consequences of higher powers and a higher life, which we may morally achieve", thought psychologist William James (quoted in Huxley 2004a: viii). Such a conception of the good as the grounds for wellbeing, and love as the mechanism by which we might be awakened to, discover and embody it, suggests a deep affinity between religious feeling, moral appeal and the life lived well. That will be another part of my argument at the end.

Kennels and palaces

There is one additional point I'd like to raise at the start, that is both philosophical and personal. The philosophical issue is raised in a parable told by the philosopher Søren Kierkegaard:

> A thinker erects an immense building, a system, a system which embraces the whole of existence and world-history etc. – and if we contemplate his personal life, we discover to our astonishment this terrible and ludicrous fact, that he himself personally does not life in this immense high-vaulted palace, but in a barn alongside of it, or in a dog kennel, or at the most in the porter's lodge. (Kierkegaard 1978: 21)

This is the great challenge for any advocate of a system of wellbeing, be it self-help, positive psychology, moral philosophy or for that matter just common sense: not whether they can describe it, or whether they believe it works, but whether they actually live it – has it become for them a way of life? It is a bit like faith. That becomes holiness not because someone confesses this or that belief but because it shines through them. What you really love becomes clear because of who you are becoming.

It was not for the first time, but I had a sense of this challenge myself relatively recently, just before starting on this book. I was in Hong Kong, visiting my brother who lives there. It is a place with an energy that is almost mad, an ebullience manifest in its skyscrapers that do not arise in regular rows as in Manhattan, but jostle like stalagmites of glass and chrome pushing up from the floor of a sun-kissed cave. The city loves many things – food, boats, horses, shops – although my brother always says that one love alone serves as a god: money.

So Hong Kong was not the place I expected to meet Thomas (I've changed his name to save him embarrassment). He lives on one of the smaller islands called Lamma: not, I think, named after the Tibetan word for teacher. Lamma makes moving at a less frenetic pace its speciality. There are no cars or high-rise buildings on the island. People walk more slowly. It is for those who want a simpler life than in the city. Thomas's house certainly achieves that. It could be described as an open-plan shack about five minutes walk along a concrete path from the harbour. It is furnished with bamboo chairs, beds on the floor and dusty books, and is surrounded by heavy banana palms, which look exotic, although as we sat drinking tea on the little lawn he had sowed beneath them, I realized they were also home to several mosquitoes.

My brother wanted me to meet Thomas because he is a spiritual man. He'd spent a few years living in India, and visited Tibet several times, along with other places on the hippie trail. I was sceptical. My philosophical antennae were on the alert for crazy New Age vibes: you can overdo it on the spirit level! I was quite taken aback. It was not just that Thomas had astute, rational criticisms to offer about his own past in pursuit of wellbeing: the tendency towards self-indulgence; the toe-dipping into Eastern traditions that can lack real discernment and commitment. And he was prepared openly to discuss them. What spoke more powerfully was that this home he had made had a powerful sense of place. It was really good to be there. There was something of wellbeing in the air. Later, I looked up some words by the seventeenth-century poet and religious writer Thomas Traherne:

> Till your spirit filleth the whole world, and the stars are your jewels; till you are as familiar with the ways of God in all ages as with your walk and table; till you are intimately acquainted with that shady nothing out of which the world was made; till you love men so as to desire their happiness with a thirst equal to the zeal of your own; till you delight in God for being good to all; you never enjoy the world. (2002: 4)

It seemed to me that Thomas had discovered how to enjoy the world. He does not live in a barn or porter's lodge alongside the palace of his ideals. He has achieved the goal of making his home the palace. I felt he'd worked out what he loved, and how to love it. His is not just a good life: in its simplicity it shows through the good in life.

I've no idea if Thomas knew how profoundly going to his house affected me. But in retrospect it prompted me to try to move beyond just discussing philosophy, religion and the good life in abstract, and to attempt to know of it more profoundly: in pursuit and practice. Thomas has been on my mind as I have been writing.

Plato knew this too. He said that real knowledge is not like water that can be poured from one vessel into another, or from one book into another. Facts, findings and rules count, although they may easily be a "mere logical understanding, a technique, a meaningless bundle of undirected skills", in the words of Karl Jaspers (2003: ch. III). For if it is wellbeing you seek, there is one central challenge: to respond to love and see how to live.

That said, there is in an Indian Sutra that makes another point: only the person who sees by themselves needs no instruction. The rest of us are dragged down and tossed about in a miasma of pains and pleasure, existing for the most part in pursuits that are lower not higher. Seeking insight into the art of wellbeing, it is to that whirl that we must therefore first turn.

1. Pleasure and pain

One half of the world cannot understand the pleasures of the other.   (Jane Austen, *Emma*)

Pleasure. It is so welcome, so immediate, so tangible, so motivating: it is its own reward. If you put sophisticated and refined pleasures on the menu of life, such as fulfilling relationships and stretching ambitions, as well as those small pleasures akin to eating chocolates, then it appears to be a no-brainer to conclude that the maximization of quality pleasure should be the central goal of wellbeing. At the very least, it just seems counterintuitive to suggest that a good life has little to do with good feeling. The assertion would seem so easy to knock down.

That is certainly what many have taken as gospel since the Enlightenment. Happiness finds its greatest delight and stimulation when enlivened by pleasure, explained Abbé Pestré, in his entry on the matter for Diderot and d'Alembert's famous eighteenth-century *Encyclopédie*. Or to put it another way, he championed the notion that perfect happiness would be a state of perpetual, quality pleasure uninterrupted by pain. He continues:

> If happiness is not enlivened from time to time by pleasure, it is not so much true happiness as a state of tranquillity, a very sorry kind of happiness indeed! If we are left in a state of lazy indolence that offers no stimulus to our activity, we cannot be happy; our desires can only be fulfilled by our being

transported out of this listlessness in which we languish. Joy must flow into the innermost recesses of our hearts, it must be stimulated by pleasant feelings, kept in motion by gentle shocks, filled with delightful variety, it must intoxicate us with a pure pleasure that nothing can spoil.

Pestré shared these assumptions with the authors of many of the treatises that were published on happiness in the eighteenth century; in the early days of modernity it was quite as blossoming an industry as it is today. He knew, of course, that perfect happiness is not practically achievable, for the reason that in reality pleasure rises and falls like a flame. Also, if it burns too brightly it burns itself out. But then, as Lord Byron wrote in *Don Juan* a few years later:

Let us have wine and women, mirth and laughter,
Sermons and soda-water the day after.

There is something profoundly compelling in the notion that a good life has much to do with physical joys and mental delights. We can be sophisticated about it, for sure. But is it not unanswerable that happiness in one way or another essentially boils down to increasing the amount of positive emotion you enjoy? Dissatisfaction and suffering are the opposite of wellbeing. We should do everything to reduce them, if not cut them out; they are so self-evidently horrid. So why might there be grounds for believing otherwise?

Oranges and apples

The cracks start to show if you turn to the individual who made the most robust case for such a sophisticated hedonism, the English philosopher Jeremy Bentham, the founding father of utilitarianism and, incidentally, the godfather of John Stuart Mill.

Bentham was convinced that whatever might be the essence of a good life, it must be a straightforward matter, for only something that is straightforward could warrant the title of the greatest good for which any human being, in their right senses, would aspire. He was not a stupid man; he knew that great minds before him had thought that the key to happiness is as elusive as answers to the riddles of the Sphinx. But he thought that the pleasure principle was so powerful, so direct an idea of wellbeing, that it could sweep all the equivocation aside.

One immediate difficulty is that there are pleasures and pleasures. The joy of reading a book is not like the buzz of dancing until dawn. The contentment of loving your spouse after thirty years of marriage is not like the thrill of being swept off your feet on a date. The risk is that before you know what you are doing, the good life is reduced to a more or less silly series of calculations about what to choose: dancing and dates or reading and marriage? In general, there is a need to assess different pleasures for happiness-as-positive-emotion to work, and establish which are likely to lead to the greatest happiness, and therefore which are the best to cultivate.

Bentham developed a quasi-scientific means of doing so, called felicific calculus. He drew up tables of pleasures and graded them one against the other. Most contemporaries thought it untenable, not least Mill. It just seemed so crude. Mill pointed out that pleasures do not vary just in intensity but also in kind— as oranges differ from apples. Or there is the issue of how one person's pleasure can be met with another's disgust: marmite, Stockhausen, gay sex – some people's stomachs turn at all three. Or take an extreme case. What about those pleasures that are evil: the torturer who delights in cruelty or the paedophile who finds comfort with children? Both might argue with conviction that acting in a way that brings them pleasure contributes to their wellbeing. That is the way they are made.

Bentham argued back that consequences count too. What people do should be assessed by their effects, not least in terms of the pleasure or pain they cause others. But this only works in a world where the consequences of actions can be seen in relative black and white. The extreme cases are the easy cases. Mostly, though, the world is a smudge of barely indistinguishable greys. What about the ordinary, frustrated individual who obtains some small satisfaction in everyday acts of humdrum vengeance? Is the offence they cause the call-centre operator worth the satisfaction they feel at venting their anger? Is the aggression they show others by pummelling the car-horn justified by the release they experience in their road-rage? Adding up the negatives and offsetting them against the positives in a ledger of utility, before settling on the best course of action, is in practice ham-fisted. Focusing so much on maximizing pleasure just seems a clumsy way to live. It is not that pleasure is bad; it is that making it the main gauge of the good life is flawed.

Put like that, there would seem to be no argument. However, pleasure is persuasive. We are sentient beings. We are also, today, consumers. That must have something to do with a good life! Sure enough, felicific calculus is making something of a come-back armed with twenty-first-century science, for there are now striking ways of making the pleasurable measurable that revive neo-Benthamite aspirations. Brain-scanners can be deployed to take direct readings of pleasure centres in the brain. Alternatively, questionnaires and experiments, along with algorithms to unravel the results, aim to distil simple but powerful truths from the complexities of what people say about the things that make them feel better or worse.

And yet is this really any more sophisticated than Bentham, for all that 4D CT scan images of grey matter responding to stimuli in real time are impressive? For example, there is a risk of circular reasoning: pleasure centres in the brain are only recognized as such because individuals have previously said they are experiencing pleasure as, say, the *nucleus accumbens* lights up. Alternatively, there is one of the Duc de la Rochefoucauld's *Maxims* to consider:

"One is never as unhappy as one thinks, nor as happy as one hopes". What we feel about wellbeing is not always the best judge. And it depends on who's asking: pollster, politician, psychologist or philosopher. It's a bit like the concern opinion pollsters have when measuring religiosity in America and secularity in Europe: people tend to answer as they think they should, church-going being thought respectable in the US and as an activity only suitable for "nutters" in the UK. The implication is that people are alienated from what they actually believe. In the case of happiness, they may struggle to ascertain what they feel. Similarly, there is good reason to presume that some people will feel happier just because someone bothered to ask.

Researchers in this area are quite conscious of these experimental hurdles. Comparative studies that cross-reference results to ensure that human guinea-pigs are being consistent is one tactic for attempting to surmount them. The problem is that even enhanced felicific calculus treats life as simpler than it is. As a rule few things in life that really matter can be accurately measured. Love blows hot and cold but not in carefully calibrated degrees. Motivations are more or less pure but usually something of a muddle in the middle. The science of measuring happiness by measuring pleasure would be a great strength if it provided a firm basis for evidence and data. It becomes a weakness if, because of the need to measure something – anything – in order to derive tangible evidence, it measures the wrong things. This is not to be against science, any more than it is to be against pleasure. It is simply to be realistic about what the science can achieve. Great strides are being made in terms of understanding how the brain works. But to be frank the advice about wellbeing that is derived from it is often just trite: people feel better when they do such things as accept they are human, simplify their lives, exercise regularly and focus on the positive. It sounds like a lesson in the bleeding obvious because all it can do is state what is, more or less, immediately apparent.

Barley cakes and water

For all that, though, pleasure is a part of happiness. So what is a good attitude to have towards it? The ancient philosopher who understood its appeal more than anyone was Epicurus. He concurred that it was the crucial issue for human beings. However, he saw that there is an inexorable logic to pleasure-seeking that is likely to undo you if you set it as how you judge your life – directly or indirectly. What did he advise? In short, if you want to live well, keep pleasure in its place.

"No pleasure is a bad thing in itself," he said, "but the things which produce certain pleasures bring troubles many times greater than the pleasures themselves" (*Principal Doctrines*, 8). He argued that if you take pleasure as your guide then, wittingly or not, you will be committed to a life pursuing its peaks. You will endorse all sorts of accumulative tendencies that turn out to be unwise. And then you will be condemned: condemned to fall repeatedly from the heights to the troughs that follow them. This will be true whether your pleasures are high- or low-minded: a melancholic dip comes after finishing a novel as surely as the "Tuesday blues" tags a weekend on Ecstasy. Down follows up like a shadow. That is true for anyone. But if the ups are more or less the only things that make life worth living for you, then you will become ensnared in a vicious cycle of increasingly intense, decreasingly satisfying hits.

This is the moody life of the teenager wedded to his or her kicks. It is that of the gourmand who bolts his food and then complains of indigestion, as the saying has it. Is that not a metaphor for our age? Coupled to that is a further point that resonates particularly powerfully today. If you live in a society in which everyone is striving for more – bigger houses, better holidays, larger pay-packets, swisher clothes – then an ethic of avarice and aggression will emerge. The competitive desire to outdo the neighbours becomes a defining characteristic of life. Keeping one step ahead of the Joneses is what you come to love because it secretly gives you more pleasure –

maybe more than a rising standard of living does itself. Hence, in a marketplace of easy, pleasurable luxuries, *unhappiness* will spread. It sounds wrong: more pleasure for all turns out not to be correlated to more happiness for all – although anyone who has been elbowed in an Ikea on a crowded Sunday morning will know that already.

The danger was understood by Adam Smith, no enemy of capitalism. In his *Theory of Moral Sentiments* he recalled an inscription on the tombstone of a man who had been ruined by the ambition that can turn the blessings of our age into a curse. The epitaph read: "I was well, I wished to be better; here I am".

The trick, Epicurus explained, is to uproot the wild pursuit of peaks and in its place allow to grow a cultivated attention that delights in whatever you happen to have. He called it *ataraxia*, or serenity, born he thought of an "obscure life", which is to say, one with enough space in it to think. It will embrace refined or spiritual goods, such as friends and, if possible, a beautiful place to live. Epicurus set up his philosophy school in a location with the enchanting name the "Garden". The Garden had the advantage of not being in the city and so away from those cutthroat, competitive compulsions that are so damaging. Epicurus explained it in his letter to his friend Menoeceus:

> So when we say that pleasure is the goal we do not mean the pleasures of the profligate or the pleasures of consumption, as some believe, either from ignorance and disagreement or from deliberate misinterpretation, but rather the lack of pain in the body and disturbance in the soul.

An Epicurean "hedonist" will be happy to make do with modest means, such as barley cakes and water. He or she might positively seek to give things up, since "wealth, if limits are not set for it, is great poverty". "Blessed are the meek" is the Christian version of this, the Greek for "blessed" here meaning happy as well as holy.

So, less is more when it comes to pleasure, lest the desire for more undermines your wellbeing. Epicurus would do away with the accumulation of things and positive emotion, and cultivate tranquillity of mind instead. In this, he was perhaps a bit like the Buddhist who practises mindfulness: the aim is not to be rid of thoughts, feelings and emotions but to notice them for what they are – mostly distractions. Something like that attention appears to have been the essence of human wellbeing for Epicurus and his followers.

The problem of pain

So Epicurus has a better way forward. But is it enough to make sense of life? The problem is that it still revolves around the matter of pleasure. He was no hedonist, as the word commonly means today. But his notion of wellbeing remained bound to its logic.

The issue can be put in this way. Might there not be cases in which pain contributes to wellbeing? For wellbeing, in real life, it is not just that the suffering that people face would always ideally be ameliorated, overcome or banished, although that is certainly the case in many situations; it is also possible, in fact likely, that some difficulties, even tragedies, are an important part of what makes us human, indeed they make us more human. In truth there is more to suffering and the life lived well than simply a desire to remove it or anaesthetize it: to push difficulties aside as if they were as much brushwood.

The imaginary pleasure machine, made famous in a thought experiment devised by the philosopher Robert Nozick (1974), is revealing in this respect. This utopian device delivers happiness by feeding you positive emotions so precisely that you cannot tell they are not real. The surprise is that, when asked, most people would not want to be plugged into it. That they are naturally resistant to this ticket to everlasting felicity has been interpreted in different ways.

Some say it implies that happiness must be based on real not artificial life, others that happiness necessitates actually making a difference not merely simulating it. However, another answer would be that people also intuitively know that a life without pain would be no life. It might be hard to define exactly why that should be. And it would not imply the perverse conclusion that the deliberate infliction of pain is good, although as any parent will know, even that principle is true on occasion. What the pleasure machine implies is that heaven, for humans, is not unalloyed joy. Life requires grit, struggle, and perhaps sometimes a singe that may scar. "What man actually needs is not a tensionless state but rather the striving and struggling for some goal worthy of him", Viktor Frankl (1959: 127) thought.

Further sense can be made of this by considering the results of research into parenting and children that shows that when parents are asked whether raising children brings them more pleasure or more pain, the answers typically hang in the balance. Parents are not sure. Now, without an understanding of struggle, the result seems somewhat quizzical. Might the message for your greater happiness be don't have kids? Intuition would suggest that something is wrong with that assessment, since children would undoubtedly be part of many people's idea of wellbeing. And indeed they are. I would say the problem is interpreting life in relation to pleasure, and therefore having trouble accommodating the necessity of pain. Asking parents about how they feel about their kids is probably simply the wrong question. Children are to do with fulfilment or love or hope, which are infinitely more complex and paradoxical aspects of life than mere pleasure, and invariably bring agonies too.

The issue of joys that come only in conjunction with sorrows can be generalized to embrace all sorts of valuable things such as struggling to read, or running a race, or suffering with a friend. And then there is love: "All other pleasures are not worth its pains", it has been said. Such experiences are as much a trial as a treat. But since any kind of meaningful life requires us to deal with other people – and if not with others then certainly with ourselves – it seems highly likely that wellbeing is inseparable from what we might call meaningful suffering, or at least the potential for suffering, which, for the human animal, gifted with the capacity to ponder the future, is inevitably part of life.

Nietzsche highlighted a related matter. He noted that times of hardship can teach people certain things and deepen their emotional lives; that is, they can improve their overall wellbeing. He put this rather well when he pointed out that pain can be a great source of wisdom. "There is as much wisdom in pain as there is in pleasure", he wrote (1974: § 318). Smarting can make you smarter.

Clearly there is such a thing as pointless suffering, such as the pain of chronic physical suffering, or the unnecessary agonies that the powerful can so easily inflict on the poor. And there is a cautionary note to sound when talking about suffering that Kierkegaard caught in a parable:

> What is a poet? An unhappy man who in his heart harbours a deep anguish, but whose lips are so fashioned that the moans and cries which pass over them are transformed into ravishing music ... And men crowd about the poet and say to him, "Sing for us soon again" – which is as much as to say, "May new sufferings torment your soul, but may your lips be fashioned as before; for the cries would only distress us, but the music, the music, is delightful." (1978: 4)

Warning heeded. But some pain is prophetic. Nietzsche continues, "That it hurts is no argument against it but is its essence". This would be true, say, of the pain caused by an injury or illness that is the early warning system of the body. Prophetic pain can be psychological too. Nietzsche tells a parable about some monkeys to make the point. He had read some research that appeared to show that monkeys can tell when the weather is going to turn bad. This is not because they have weather forecasts or can read the clouds, but because they feel changes in pressure or the build-up of electrostatic charge in the sky. They feel these atmospheric effects not as objective natural events but as similar to their experience of an enemy drawing near, that is, as fear. Wise pain: find shelter. Nietzsche concludes that there can be a value for human beings in not turning your back on fear but embracing it, even refining your sensitivity towards it. Then, when a storm is approaching, you are able to rise to the challenge and see yourself through to the other side, all the stronger for it.

To reflect on the apparently growing experience that people have of depression is to reflect again on this question. In his book *The New Black: Mourning, Melancholia and Depression*, the psychoanalyst and writer Darian Leader explores how we might be profoundly misconstruing our understanding of depression and in a sense causing that depression. The key error is to refuse depression a place in life. This happens because it doesn't fit with the modern image of what it is to be a human being: autonomous, amenable to science, productive to the economy, and the like. So we adopt the biochemical approach to treating it, essentially mechanistically, as if it were an infection like a sore throat, or a period of sub-optimal functioning to be corrected like retuning a car.

This, though, is to seek to remove the suffering rather than to understand it; taking pills to paper over the cracks. For depression might be telling us something about ourselves, and our wellbeing. According to Leader, it speaks of the melancholia and mourning that follows the experience of losses in life, be that because of death, the end of relationships or disillusionment. He suggests that the reason depression is on the rise, apart from what he identifies as the dark promotion of the "condition" by drug companies, is because as a society we are becoming so bad at mourning. We are losing a crucial skill for our wellbeing. Rising levels of depression should not be responded to with yet more pills, but by listening to that depression: it's perhaps a kind of protest against the conditions – emotional and spiritual, not material – that people are being forced to live in.

Spiritual suffering

A different way of embracing the problem of pain is to develop the capacity to manage or transcend it, as opposed to wanting to remove it. Consider the moment in *Zen and the Art of Motorcycle Maintenance* when Robert M. Pirsig describes how his protagonist, Phaedrus, couldn't keep up with some pilgrims who were climbing a Himalayan peak, although he was younger and presumably fitter than all of them. The issue was not just that they were able to enjoy the climb in a way he could not. Phaedrus's motivational problems stemmed from the fact that he could not share in the spiritual worth that the pilgrims associated with the ascent. He became overwhelmed by a question that did not bother them: "What's the point?" Thus, when the effort became too much, he fell aside. For them, though, it never was much a matter of pleasure or pain to start with. Their focus was on the "holiness of the mountain": "each footstep was an act of devotion, an act of submission to this holiness" (1974: 205).

Just how transcending pain might be possible is explored by the Dalai Lama in his bestseller, *The Art of Happiness*, co-written with Howard C. Cutler. Throughout the book pleasure and happiness are prised apart. For example, when faced with a decision in life, a useful Buddhist practice is to ask whether you might do something because of the pleasure it would bring or because it would make you happier. There is a difference, and the implication is that the latter way of assessing a choice is better.

The Dalai Lama expresses this in a religious frame by referring to suffering as a spiritual practice. It enables empathy with other people who are also suffering. This deepening of compassion partly has an instrumental outcome when it increases the resolve to do what is possible to stop the unnecessary causes of suffering in the world. However, it also sees suffering as having intrinsic worth since it is an opportunity to identify with others. Suffering can be an experience of connection and, given that relatedness is a fundamental human value, thereby understood within the context of wellbeing. In the Christian tradition, in which Christ suffered and died on the cross, this takes on another sense: suffering is an identification with God. Again, it is worth stressing that this is not the glorification of suffering *per se*; Christians, like Buddhists, would agree with humanists that it is supremely good to ease suffering when possible. Rather, it is a recognition of the meaning that suffering can have. As Frankl, who suffered in the Nazi camps, wrote: "That is why man is even ready to suffer on the condition, to be sure, that his suffering has a meaning" (2004: 113).

Stark as it is to confess in black and white, it just seems to be the case that the removal of all suffering from the world would neither automatically enhance our lives nor straightforwardly improve our wellbeing. In ways that are not always clear, something of our humanity would perish along with the pain. The core issue, it seems, is not actually one of increasing pleasure and decreasing pain. It is pointless suffering that offends, meaninglessness that truly causes despair. This observation moves us on to new territory, and perhaps a more profound determinant of wellbeing. Pleasure matters. But meaning matters more.

2. The meaning dimension

Where more is meant than meets the ear.

(Milton, "Il Penseroso")

So human beings are creatures for whom meaning is a crucial, a characteristic, part of their wellbeing. You see people seeking it every day in all kinds of ways. Religion, science and the arts all invest heavily in meaning-related notions, such as: that there are ways of living in the world that make more sense than others; that there are patterns to be discerned in nature that express deep order; that it is not just facts that count but values. Even those who would not think of themselves as religious, scientific or artistic engage in a meaning-seeking activity day and night: they use language to communicate, to shape their world, to make things happen, to reveal that which can and, conversely, that which cannot be said. Language might be called that which "raises to significance". As Dominican priest and philosopher Herbert McCabe wrote in *The Good Life*: "Language is the nervous system of the human community. It is the context for meaning" (2005: 67).

There are, I think, broadly two ways of thinking about meaning. The first defines it as having purpose, and ideally a purpose of your own choosing. According to this view, it doesn't much matter what pursuit it is that provides you with a sense of purpose, so long as it falls within the bounds of social respectability. But it should provide one key facility: delay of gratification. This is necessary to overcome the allure of pleasure that otherwise demands its own reward, and demands it now. The greater the purpose, the greater its capacity to withhold on immediate gratifications – with the promise of even greater reward later. To think about meaning in this way is to treat it like a tool that can shift your perspective to the long term. Studying for exams may seem pointless now, but you suffer it so as to gain qualifications that will be useful later. Working the nine-to-five may be pretty mind-numbing, but there is always the pay to look forward to. With this approach to meaning, you are prepared to forestall what you feel in the present in return for rewards that should be realized in the future. It is an approach that is instrumental: it is not what you are doing that is meaningful but you do it because of what will be delivered to you.

But this is to consider only one sense of meaning, and the lesser one at that. It is utilitarian and that is different from meaning that is innate, inherent, intrinsic. This is meaning in a second sense. It is meaning that you sense regardless of what you are doing. Indeed, this kind of meaning often only comes through when the background noise of incessant activity stops. "Only love has meaning"; "The church is where I find meaning"; "Science offers me a sense of meaning": here, love, the church, the study of nature do not themselves provide meaning, they *reveal* meaning. Meaning, as it were, shines through them. This is not meaning that we create. It is meaning that one has to be ready to see. This is why someone who is convinced that life is meaningless will find no consolation in anything that you suggest they do. What they are troubled by is meaning as an existential issue. A project might distract someone in such desperate straits; it might bury their sadness. But they would neither work to make meaning nor be in a place to find it. They would work to forget that they lived.

The fundamental quality of intrinsic meaning is that it is good because it is good in itself: you can say that its worth has nothing to do with you. Moreover, that conviction would remain even if it delivered nothing in terms of increasing happiness. A cause that carried great meaning might demand serious suffering or the ultimate sacrifice. But it would be worth it: not in the sense of being worthwhile but of having significance. Intrinsic meaning is like saying: better to have loved and lost, than never to have loved at all. For to have loved is to have tasted something that is good in itself. That taste might have been agony but it is transformative; life can never look the same again because the person who has loved has incarnated, for a while, something of supreme value.

It is this sense of meaning that I suspect Aristotle would have thought lay behind by the activities he recommends in the eudaimonistic life, although it should be noted that the contemporary way of talking about meaningfulness would have been alien to him; he lived in a world in which meaning was not in crisis, for everything he saw around him, even water and stones, had a purpose. He discusses *eudaimonia* in his *Nicomachean Ethics* and, as the chapters progress, examines many of the specific activities that could help an ancient Greek to flourish. They will practice the virtues: loving courageously, befriending honestly, giving generously and so on. But the virtues are not an end in themselves. Rather, they cultivate a character that is then open to the possibility of innate meaning. An individual with such a character is like the archer who, although perhaps far from his target, trains himself to keep it steadily in view. Or like a flautist whose habitual long hours of practising and ability to deliver a charismatic performance stem from a whole way of life that is geared to developing her excellence. For Aristotle, the activity that crowns them all is that of contemplation. Contemplation is the ability to see through to what has meaning in itself. *Eudaimonia* is completed in a profound sense of unmediated meaningfulness, although again it is a little anachronistic to put it like that. Aristotle himself talked about seeing truth.

The question of flow

In many contemporary books on happiness, the state of being in flow is presented as a sort of contemporary equivalent of Aristotle's active contemplation. Otherwise known as "being in the zone", the research the concept comes from describes it as being immersed in an activity that challenges but does not confound you. You feel that you are making progress, if with some effort. It might be experienced in a sport, in a conversation, in a performance. It is observed that people in flow lose all sense of the passage of time and know they are alive. It is a peak experience coinciding with peak performance; present and future benefits merge. There is no longer any opposition between pleasure now or later. Irrelevant is the old mantra "no pain, no gain". Flow is presented as so desirable because it is having your cake and eating it! It has instrumental value because it gives you a sense of purpose.

There is something important about flow for wellbeing. It is mean-ingful. And yet, when I first read such descriptions of the experience something struck me as odd. I compared them with what I took to be my own experiences of flow, notably when reading and writing. That can be intense, in the sense that in my focused concentration the rest of the world closes down. All kinds of thoughts and connec-tions emerge during these periods that would seem impossible to conjure up during normal waking hours: what novelists report as characters "writing themselves". However, when it comes to being meaningful it is not the matter of feeling that I have a purpose that comes to the fore. Flow, if anything, brings with it the thoroughly ambivalent feelings of being spent. Often, I am not sure whether what I have been doing has been worthwhile at all; I certainly have days when I would not want to see my output in print. Instead, at base, it is a sense that I am pursuing what I have to that matters.

So it is not the flow that is desirable. Rather, flow happens because I am engaged in something that I want to do. It is, as it were, a by-product. If I sought it directly I doubt whether I would find it; in fact, I'm not sure how I could seek it directly. Moreover, with all the effort that seems to be involved when flow happens, it is far from clear that I'd want it for its own sake. There are much easier pleasures!

I looked for descriptions of flow elsewhere. There is the life of the artist, as described by Kandinsky in his *Concerning the Spiritual in Art*. Art was a vocation for him, its task being "harmonizing the whole", and in this way he thought of it as spiritual. It sounds as though such a life would be a prime candidate for peak experience combined with peak performance. But this all-encompassing task has a substantial downside. In fact, Kandinsky talks about the artist's life in the language of suffering and fear as much as anything else:

> The artist is not born to a life of pleasure. He must not live idle;
> he has a hard work to perform, and one which often proves a
> cross to be borne. He must realize that his every deed, feeling,
> and thought are raw but sure material from which his work is
> to arise, and he is free in art but not in life.   (1977: 54)

Alternatively, I recall the five-times Olympic gold medal winning rower Steve Redgrave being asked, on retiring, to describe what it had been like to be at the top of his sport. The interviewer was looking for an insight into a wholly absorbed life. Maybe he was wondering if he should take up rowing to enjoy something of the same. Redgrave did not oblige. It was as if he had not understood what was being asked, as if he'd never thought about it like that. His pursuit of rowing excellence had been more like a form of madness to him: restrictive diets, early rising, the physical torture of the race. It was precisely a life in which there was no gain without pain. So why had he done it? He couldn't really say, only he knew that something innate had driven him to it.

Then I found these two accounts of "flowful" periods in the life of the philosopher Karl Popper, taken from his autobiography, *Unended Quest*. In the first, during the middle part of his life, he does link flow with finding happiness on settling in England. His word for flow is the Greek word *autark*, literally translated as sufficient in oneself, and carrying the implication of being fully absorbed and acting instinctively. Popper writes:

> I have worked hard, and I have often got deep into insoluble difficulties. But I have been most happy in finding new problems, in wrestling with them, and in making some progress. This, or so I feel, is the best life ... It is a completely restless life, but it is highly self-contained – *autark* in Plato's sense, although no life, of course, can be fully *autark* ... I have been, I suspect, the happiest philosopher I have met.   (2002: 144)

However, contrast that period with another, which was also characterized by what could be called flow. It was from an earlier time in his life, and this time what is striking is that, although flowful, any sense of happiness was entirely off the cards:

> Although the years after the First World War were grim for most of my friends and also for myself, it was an exhilarating time. Not that we were happy. Most of us had no prospects and no plans. We lived in a very poor country in which civil war was endemic, flaring up in earnest from time to time. We were often depressed, discouraged, disgusted. But we were learning, our minds were active and growing. We were reading ravenously, omnivorously; debating, changing our opinions, studying, sifting critically, thinking. We listened to music, went tramping in the beautiful Austrian mountains, and dreamt of a better, healthier, simpler, and more honest world.   (*Ibid.*: 39)

These reflections suggest to me that flow is certainly something real. But to think of it as if it were good because it provides happiness is wrong. It misses what is really at the heart of the matter; it focuses on something that may or may not be present and is not key. What really counts is to have discovered a devotion, a passion for something that has intrinsic meaning.

So something has gone wrong in books about happiness that talk about flow and therefore recommend the pursuit of it. What they actually do is put the cart before the horse. Consider the research that indicates that people with a strong sense of meaning in life often identify that awareness with holding religious beliefs. A crude interpretation of this well-observed fact might, therefore, suggest that a good life requires taking up church-going. However, that would not be right, non-church-goers might be glad to learn. For religious people are not believers because they plan to be happier; they are religious because they have an experience of the divine or a sense of the infinite – God is the name they give to that which they find absolutely meaningful and therefore they go to church. Similarly, people who make great sacrifices in life, and thereby find another source of goodness, do not make that commitment for the purpose of being happy. Someone who was, say, to sell everything and give to the poor because they thought it would increase their wellbeing, could be sure of one thing: they would find the experience horrible, their new way of life unbearable. The prescription would not deliver on its promise.

In fact, the psychologist who first defined flow, Mihály Csíkszentmihályi, subsequently refused to offer people advice on "how to flow". He was wise, for asking "the how" of flow undermines the possibility of the state. No longer would you simply read ravenously, omnivorously: debate, change your opinions, study, sifting critically, think – to recall Popper's description. In focusing on the flow you would fall right out of the zone, if you ever achieved it!

Csíkszentmihályi perhaps understood this because the same thing is exactly what happens when researchers examine flow. Typically, such research involves experience sampling methods, or ESMs. Researchers beep individuals on pagers at random moments in the day and ask them to record what they are thinking and feeling there and then. But if they were "in flow" at the time, the experiment, inevitably, interrupts it. It might be thought of as the flow researcher's Heisenberg uncertainty moment. It is a telling one. Interfering in the experiences collapses them, as the probability wave function of the electron collapses when it is observed. You never actually get an electron. You see a particle or a wave depending on how you are looking. Similarly, the studies never actually see flow. The science of the concept is condemned to hearing but an echo.

The danger of self-help

Too instrumental an approach to wellbeing, as in the advice to go for flow, has an unfortunate side-effect: it nurtures self-centeredness. For when people organize their lives to increase their happiness, they also, perhaps unwittingly, practise becoming self-absorbed. They risk reorientating themselves in a way that assumes that the world serves to deliver on their happiness. What do they learn to love? Themselves.

Of course, there are individuals for whom a lack of self-love is pathological. They will never live well without a more robust sense of themselves; they need to nurture *amour-propre*. And it is also the case that the wiser self-help books warn against the risk of indulging narcissism. They include exercises, say, in showing gratitude or being philanthropic, pointing out that all the research on wellbeing shows that these activities are vital for sustained contentment. I'm not sure, though, that it is enough: it repeats the mistake of putting the cart before the horse. For in presenting the care of others as activities for your happiness, altruism and gratitude cease to be valuable for their own sake. They become a series of techniques aimed at your self-interest.

The problem is that sight has been lost of intrinsic meaning. These qualities are not being considered because they matter in their own right. Rather, it is as strong indicators of happiness that they are being encouraged. This doesn't matter when it comes to activities such as cooking a steak, driving a car or tying your laces: all handy things to be able to do in life. But when it comes to things that have intrinsic value, self-centredness becomes self-defeating. You stop giving of yourself and take for yourself.

A comparison with Aristotle's approach to happiness is illuminating. When he wrote about *eudaimonia*, his aim was to explore the matter and capture its essence as clearly as he could. He even went so far as to give talks on the subject: the *Nicomachean Ethics* are probably his lecture notes, saved for posterity by his enterprising son. Aristotle's strategy for nurturing wisdom on the matter was to offer his thoughts and suggest what he thought was the best way of life. But he knew that if it became too prescriptive, his prescriptions themselves would become the goal, and would detract from the pursuit of the good in life. The secret ingredient was the practical wisdom that comes from actually living. That can't be captured on the page, or in an exercise. The page and the exercise must serve the good. To put it in a modern idiom, he sought to deepen people's self-understanding and offer them something to love, not merely deliver prescriptions.

Friendship provides another good case and develops the point. There is a story that is nowadays often told to account for its worth and origins. It is borrowed from evolutionary psychology and the observation that in certain versions of the game known as the prisoner's dilemma it pays the individual to cooperate with others. Similarly, in games of tit-for-tat, a winning strategy is to do to others as you would have them do to you. This has been labelled "reciprocal altruism", after its apparent similarity with the so-called Golden Rule: the idea that your own best interests are served if you agree to help others. The presumption is that our hunter-gatherer ancestors evolved the trait since it better served the preservation of the genes belonging to the individuals that expressed it. Moreover, to reward the reciprocal altruism of an individual, which after all might cost him or her a temporary set-back in their wellbeing, evolution also endowed people who make such sacrifices with a deeper sense of purpose. Hence, for example, we admire people who "do the right thing", although it demands much of them.

There is, in fact, a big question to ask about whether the evolutionary account of reciprocal altruism is even science, let alone whether it is correct. The biologist Stephen Jay Gould used to call the claim that we have such and such a feature on account of what it gained for our hunter-gatherer ancestors shaggy dog stories. His point was that Darwinism has led to all sorts of human characteristics supposedly being "explained" by saying that they are the result of evolutionary adaptation when, in fact, evolutionary theory is simply not up to that level of explanation at all. It works brilliantly at the level of physical characteristics, but there is little reason to think it works that well at the psychological level.

There is even less reason to think it works when it comes to ethical concerns. Darwin himself speculated on the possibility of evolutionary origins for "aiding fellows". In *The Descent of Man*, he proposed that people might have learnt that giving to others leads to receiving in return. Such a practice might become a habit that led to sympathy of character. However, he was uncomfortable with the implication that such friendship stemmed from a "low motive", from the cold calculation implicit in the mutual scratching of backs. Further, this instrumental account of friendship seemed to leave no space for friendship in which there is no need for an exchange of benefits: the friendship that loves another human being simply for who they are in themselves, because they are lovely. Aristotle, for one, had argued that this was the quintessential kind of friendship. Far more than the instrumental kind, it contributed to the eudaimonistic life. He also argued that it is because we ascribe intrinsic moral value to this excellent friendship, as he called it, that instrumental friendship, although of lesser value, can be appreciated as valuable to a significant degree: it reminds us, as it were, what the best friendship can be like.

Morally speaking, what evolutionary psychology does, then, is again get it the wrong way round. It encourages the how-to-win-friends-and-influence-people approach; watch your friends disappear as they sense that the reason for your affection is what it does for you! It is not for nothing that the founders of the great religions taught what Ignatius of Loyola prayed:

To give and not to count the cost
To fight, and not to heed the wounds;
To toil and not to seek for rest;
To labour and not to ask for any reward.

("Prayer for Generosity")

This is tough. It requires real sacrifice, not just a trade-off. It is an ideal that most rarely live up to, which is why saints are so valuable: those rare individuals who enable ordinary mortals to hold on to ideals, like those of excellent friendship. But it is the highest embodiment of compassion: the loss of concern for yourself in the empathic identification with another. It is to know why compassion has intrinsic worth. It is to find, and give yourself to, innate meaning.

I think that this fault adds to explaining why much of self-help comes across as so ephemeral. Its pragmatism is often lauded: look, the research shows what works! It is as if our culture is turning to science to tell us what has intrinsic meaning, because we can't trust the old ways, but the science can't actually provide the means to tell us. Its utilitarian methodology makes for utilitarian advice and that can't go as deep as we need to, as we need to for wellbeing. Relying so much on pure science is rather like the man who dropped his keys at night and spent a long time looking for them but only under the street lamp. When a passer-by commented that they might have fallen in the shade or dark near the wall or under a tree, the man retorted that the only place he could look was in the light and so that is what he would do. If wellbeing also has to do with negative emotion and is not much amenable to scientific investigation because it has to do with a commitment to values not a discovery of facts, then it will be necessary to devise other means of investigation, other ways of understanding what it is to live and live well.

Passing happiness

I wonder whether a large part of the problem has to do with the word "happiness" itself. There is a question to ask of it: has it been dumbed down too far? Perhaps it can no longer bear the weight that is required if it is to be taken as the chief goal of human life. In this happiness could be similar to a word like "myth". In a bygone age, a myth was an event that supposedly happened once, although its real significance transcended time; to understand its meaning it had to be imaginatively interpreted. Hence myths were endlessly retold tales that revealed fundamental truths about the human condition. What, though, is a myth today? Little more than a questionable story.

Or take the word "virtue". To the ancient philosophers, virtue was that knitting together of a person's character, beliefs, habits and skilfulness at living well, with the aim of revealing the good in life. To talk of a virtuous person today more often than not implies that they are a prude.

The same erosion of richness can be seen to have happened with the word happiness. Aristotle's word, *eudaimonia*, not only implies a connection with divine goodness, it carried strong associations of human flourishing that have a distinct link to intrinsic meaning: the eudaimonistic person is someone who does good things, meaning wise and moral and is good. *Eudaimonia*, Aristotle says, is "an activity of the soul in accordance with excellence". There were other facets of excellence that sound quite strange today. He continues: "Moreover this activity must occupy a complete lifetime; for one swallow does not make spring, nor does one fine day; and similarly one day or a brief period of happiness does not make a man supremely blessed and happy" (1, 1098a 16–20). Hence, the Greeks used to say, no one can tell whether they are "happy" until they lie on their death bed and can survey the whole of their three scores years and ten.

These excellences may be of character, like courage and generosity, or intellect, like knowledge and good judgement. It is possible that such activities may incidentally bring about what we think of as happiness. They equally possibly might not. For Aristotle does not primarily recommend a certain way of life because of what he expects it will deliver for the person concerned. Rather, he recommends it because he believes it is itself constitutive of what is good.

And what does happiness mean today? Often little more than positive emotion, boosted by whatever works for you. The point is made in the chilly parable of Aldous Huxley's novel of a dystopian future, *Brave New World*. At one point, the Controller is censoring a book, and signs it off as not to be published.

A pity, he thought, as he signed his name. But once you began admitting explanations in terms of purpose – well, you didn't know what the result might be. It was the sort of idea that might easily recondition the more unsettled minds among the higher castes – make them lose their faith in happiness as the Sovereign Good and take to believing, instead, that the goal was somewhere beyond, somewhere outside the present human sphere; that the purpose of life was not

43

the maintenance of wellbeing, but some intensification and refining of consciousness, some enlargement of knowledge. Which was, the Controller reflected, quite possibly true.

(2004b: 154)

If happiness as a concept has become pallid, then the word "wellbeing" perhaps still carries real vigour. The two are often used interchangeably, as Huxley just did. But there is value in teasing them apart in order to draw attention to what is missed when the attention is dominated by the thinner philological cousin. Intuitively this makes sense. I was recently involved in the launch of a new project with an organization called Business in the Community. The aim is to promote the corporate care of employees, partly because staff with poor health lose companies lots of money, but also because there is a moral imperative to do something about what is a serious problem. Research shows that well over half of employees suffer from stress at work, well over a third from depression, and close to a quarter have panic attacks: the statistics paint a picture of sickness not success. What is noteworthy is that Business in the Community did not describe their campaign as an initiative to promote happiness in the workplace: they opted for the word wellbeing. This was partly because while work should be rewarding, to reduce that to saying work should make employees happy seems too reductive; staff would laugh at the suggestion, although that would at least have the benefit of a few minutes worth of positive emotion.

Wellbeing is a useful word because it is relatively unfamiliar. *The Oxford Dictionary of Quotations* has dozens of entries for happiness and happy. There is not a single one for wellbeing. It is not even clear how to spell it: wellbeing or well-being? Similarly, in spoken English it is not straightforwardly obvious how to use the word. You can say, "I am happy", but what would the equivalent construction be in relation to wellbeing? "I have wellbeing", is awkward. It is as if wellbeing forces us to use it indirectly: a linguistic pause that might be an advantage, given the need to think laterally.

In terms of its meaning, wellbeing embraces notions of health, contentment and flourishing. It includes psychological growth as well as physical welfare. It has an individual and a community aspect; since we are social animals, not isolated individuals, our wellbeing will have to embrace that of others. It necessitates asking what is best for someone, and not just in relation to instrumental things such as pleasures or strengths, cultivated in order to achieve happiness, but things that are of intrinsic worth such as virtue or understanding or that which is good. This is found within the word with its combination of "well" – like "well-beloved" or "well-spent" or "well-tuned" – and that most elemental expression, "being".

Another group of associations can highlight some useful reflections in a different way. Anyone who reads lifestyle magazines will know that wellbeing is typically used to refer to matters connected with the body. "Wellbeing" is the section that deals with losing weight, taking exercise or improving looks. My newspaper has a wellbeing supplement: today it includes articles on skiing, sunbathing and "superfoods". Similarly, out of the current bestselling books with wellbeing in their title, eight out of ten are guides on dieting, health or exercise. Bodily wellbeing dominates this list, if often linked with a desire for fame, beauty and cash.

What is interesting is that there is more to this corporeal preoccupation than might first meet the eye. I think it reflects the crisis about higher flourishing. The rough idea is that if the notion of transcendence seems problematic in a secular, pluralistic world, this does not mean that the human desire for transcendence has disappeared. Instead it is displaced in an attempt to transcend – as in overcome – that which is indisputably tangible to us, namely, the fleshy business of being an ultimately failing physical body.

If that is right then the widespread concern for wellbeing conceived of in predominantly physical terms might be better thought of as welfare, as in "welfare state". It might be argued that this is too narrow, welfare being about bureaucratic matters such as the provision of services for citizens, or the money and manpower required to avoid poverty, poor health, crime and other social threats to quality of life. However, people talk quite naturally about the welfare of plants or the environment, and less naturally about their wellbeing, for the good of plants, unlike humans, does not include a meaning dimension. It should be added that welfare is undoubtedly good to have, and work for. Indeed, it could be the case that you need to sort out people's welfare before they can really attend to their wellbeing, although notwithstanding that there are levels of poverty and oppression that clearly crush human beings, the general principle of one before the other is a little formulaic, I feel: to say that the relatively poor cannot flourish as human beings is to ignore the fact that being relatively rich is no guarantee of it! Is it going too far to suggest the situation could be quite the opposite? Instead, wellbeing can run in parallel with material matters. It might refer to that which is spiritually enlightening, more than physically invigorating, although the two aren't mutually exclusive.

Contemporary philosophy has suggested another take on the matter. Wellbeing, some have said, consists in rationally ordered desires, that is, desires that are not self-contradictory and so not self-undermining. Or it is the need to have goals and the means to pursue them. Or simply the possession of certain things, such as personal freedom or loving relationships. Such insights succeed in expanding the notion of wellbeing beyond the quality of life that revolves around bodies and pleasures. However, they fall short in two areas: their focus on the individual and their fragmented conception of life. This repeats the worries about instrumentality and value. For example, the philosophical needs-based approach to wellbeing can also treat relationships not as relationships but as sources of emotional support for the self-centred individual; that is to say, it risks seeing friends and family as "service providers".

Alternatively, the well-made life as one constituted by rational desires or sensible goals comes to be viewed as a series of isolated decisions or projects, to do this or achieve that. The language makes it sound as if an individual's wellbeing depends on training up a kind of internal management team that is charged with maximizing the individual's chances of succeeding in the marketplace of life.

Aristotle throws a better light on a philosophical account of wellbeing. He famously said that human beings were "political animals", meaning not that we are scheming, but that we are sociable creatures for whom the good life is best cultivated in a *polis* or community. He noticed that other animals thrive when they live together too: what swarms and packs and herds bring to bees and wolves and cows is sustenance, security and sex. Community supports this welfare side of life for human beings as well: using the Greek word for life that implies "animal living", what Aristotle called *zoē*.

However for human beings, community is vital for other reasons. It secures the side of life that seeks fulfilment and contentment; that pursues the longings not just of the body but of the heart and spirit; that brings forth human institutions and cultural traditions of which animals have no inkling – in religion, science and the arts. It makes meaning possible. It is essential for language. Everything from literature to liturgy, from exploration to enlightenment, depends on communal living. It is these elements that suggest to us that a life may not only be lived, but well lived. Aristotle used another Greek word for such life, *bios*. It refers to these deeper aspirations, this specifically human flourishing. We only have one word for life, but *bios* might be designated for us by wellbeing.

In fact, I suspect we might do well simply to forget happiness. There is a large part of me that feels it is better to push the question of what makes you feel up or down to one side. It will take care of itself. Needless to say, this is hard to do. The difficulty is that a commitment to it is deeply engrained in the Western way of life. This perhaps explains why, for most people, a serious questioning of what really matters only begins with a jolt: when, say, they have a baby, lose a partner, become ill, or gain a religion. Only then can they seriously ask the big questions of life.

It was as the Stoics said: a first step towards wellbeing – towards the reorientation of our attention in the direction of the good in life – can only be taken when false assumptions and wrong intuitions are thoroughly unlearnt. This is partly an intellectual process, although what counts is not learning but a change of heart. It is philosophy aimed not so much at clear thinking as the compelling articulation of a different way of life. The goal is a transformed consciousness of the world, not only an increase in scientific knowledge. The best philosophy is, as it were, a kind of talking cure: talking in, around and through a subject so that, first mind, then spirit, and finally body take it on. Thought as therapy. The real issue emerges, said Jaspers, "whenever men achieve awareness" (Jaspers 2003: 8).

In short, the pursuit of happiness has become a distraction, a wrong turning, a mistake. Perhaps it never was the real issue. For Aristotle, a dying hero and an exhausted artist have wellbeing in a way that a happy thief who is never caught or an exultant tyrant who dies in his own bed could never have. The hero and artist have had not just a good life, but have understood something of the good in life.

So wellbeing is a better word because it draws attention to the centrality of meaning. However, that alone is not enough. For meaning itself forces us to ask the question: what is good? This, I think, moves the discussion on again. In turn, it pushes us towards the matter of the transcendent. The connection was obvious for the ancients. The good, like the truth, was ultimately a perception that only the gods could enjoy. However, humans could touch the transcendent because of, as Aristotle put it, "the divine within us" (*Nicomachean Ethics*, 1177a17): the capacity for higher flourishing. They had faith that it was possible for human beings to share in it, if someone lives aright.

And yet, even the secular Mill, in rejecting the utilitarian philosophy of his godfather Bentham, found himself moving towards something pretty close to the transcendent. As he explains in his *Autobiography*, he decided that happiness (he could still use the word) rests on refocusing your life "on the happiness of others, on the improvement of mankind, even on some art or pursuit, followed not as a means, but as itself an ideal end" (1989: 117). These activities take you out of yourself, show you the world in a different light, move you off the instrumental and into the valuable – and thereby that which is intrinsically good. Our question has changed again: if meaning matters on what does it rest today?

3. Turning to the transcendent

Is man an ape or an angel? Now I am on the side of the
angels.   (Benjamin Disraeli)

It was the Enlightenment that caused the confusion. To many then,
it came to seem that human beings no longer need to strive for the
heavenly city because heaven was becoming a place on earth. They
could be forgiven for imagining that as fantastic progress was being
made in science. The beneficent world of modernity no longer
seemed to belong to God or his priests, or require anything that
was out of human reach. The notion of higher flourishing, nurtured
in religion, seeking transcendence, was dismissed: human wellbeing is of humankind's own making! There emerged what Charles
Taylor calls "exclusive humanism": the conviction that the location
of meaning is not found in anything beyond human comprehension. Taylor writes:

> Exclusive humanism closes the transcendence window, as
> though there were nothing beyond. More, as though it weren't
> an irrepressible need of the human heart to open that window,
> and first look, and go beyond. As though feeling this need
> were the result of a mistake, an erroneous worldview, bad
> conditioning, or worse, some pathology.   (2007: 638)

Coupled to that came a sense of entitlement that this-worldly
happiness was a right, or at least, to recall the American Declaration

of Independence, something that everyone has a right to pursue. That led to something else: an expectation, that each, in his or her own way, should enjoy the pleasures the world can offer. The ground was set for the happiness industry to be born with its self-help programmes and instrumental techniques for achieving it. Indeed, happiness became not only a right but almost a duty. Hence, in contrary mood, George Bernard Shaw could quip: "But a lifetime of happiness! No man alive could bear it: it would be hell on earth". It came to sound quite exhausting.

In fact, there was some truth in Bernard Shaw's quip. For many now think that the Enlightenment was actually shot through with ambivalence in terms of the happiness it achieved for its adherents. "Historians of European culture are in substantial agreement that in the late sixteenth and early seventeenth centuries, something like a mutation in human nature took place", Lionel Trilling (1972) wrote. For Yi-Fu Tuan, autonomy – one of the Enlightenment's greatest values – comes with: "isolation, loneliness, a sense of disengagement, a loss of natural vitality and of innocent pleasure in the givenness of the world, and a feeling of burden because reality has no meaning other than what a person chooses to impart to it" (quoted in Ehrenreich 2007: 140).

This explains why exclusive humanism has struggled with how to re-establish firm foundations for meaning. One set of ideas that emerged was particularly dark. They manifested themselves in the turbulent and violent episodes that came to dominate the history of the twentieth century, namely, the revolutionary fervour of totalitarianism, communism and fascism. These political movements might be referred to as forms of anti-religion. They look now like a recipe for ill-being, although for those caught up in their aura they seemed like salvation itself. What they offered the individual were substitutes for higher flourishing within a purely immanent political frame. When submitted to, they took the individual out of themselves in a greater although thoroughly worldly cause. In his essay "Notes on Nationalism" (1945), George Orwell describes it in this way: "The habit of identifying oneself with a single nation or other unit, placing it beyond good and evil and recognising no other duty than that of advancing its interests".

He continues: "The abiding purpose of every nationalist is to secure more power and more prestige, NOT for himself but for the nation or other unit in which he has chosen to sink his own individuality". That this is a perverse kind of transcendence shows itself in how nationalism mimics the characteristics of submission to a divinity, although one that is really a demon. Orwell says that the nationalist:

> persuades himself that [his side] IS the strongest, and is able to stick to his belief even when the facts are overwhelmingly against him. Nationalism is power-hunger tempered by self-deception. Every nationalist is capable of the most flagrant dishonesty, but he is also – since he is conscious of serving something bigger than himself – unshakeably certain of being in the right. (*Ibid.*)

This kind of exclusive humanism finds its bastard twin in militant religion that believes in a genuinely other-worldly transcendence showing itself in this world as the God of righteous vengeance and terror. The natural milieu of such movements is again the political, a sphere in which the individual can sacrifice themselves to a higher cause, quite literally so in the phenomenon of suicide bombing. Needless to say, although it is presented by its adherents as such, this too is not a recipe for wellbeing.

Friends and causes

There is another side to exclusive humanism that has tried to reformulate wellbeing positively. It might be said to reinvent the transcendent within the bounds of the human world: a kind of immanent-transcendence. For example, it focuses meaning on human relationships. Thinkers in this mode might borrow from Aristotle to do so, dropping his references to the divine. They could take the definition of friendship that he provides in the *Nicomachean Ethics*: that the friend is "another self". These two words set up a kind of decentring resonance. At the most obvious level, the friend is another self in the sense that you see yourself mirrored in your friend. "To like and dislike the same things, that is indeed true friendship", opined the Roman historian Sallust (*The War with Catiline*, 20.4).

A kind of transcendent element comes in because friendship also connects my individuality with something other than myself, namely, another human being. C. S. Lewis thought that this sense of connection was the essence of friendship: it is the astonishing moment when two people, sharing a thought or experience, realize that they see it in exactly the same way: "What? You too? I thought I was the only one". This realization has a kind of objective existence since it wholly belongs neither to one nor the other. In that moment, it is as if the friends step out of themselves and mutually dwell in an independent space. Moreover, it is good to be there. In that instant they understand something of wellbeing.

This deeper sense of friendship is one in which the closest friend becomes part of who you take yourself to be. You become soulmates, in contemporary parlance, basking in each other's reflected glory, knowing what the other will say even as they say it, two halves in all things. Aristotle had a particularly dramatic way of expressing this fusion: when asked what a friend is, he replied, "One soul inhabiting two bodies".

A similar taste of transcendence will be known by anyone who has been in love. That comes with an awareness that your psychological self is not contained within the limits of your own individuality but is to some degree or other shared with the person you love.

It is as if it hovers in between you. Hence lovers love to be physically intimate, again feeling two becoming one.

Nietzsche is one exclusive humanist who recognized this dynamic, which is remarkable since he was deeply sceptical of the notion of transcendence and empathy. He believed that when transcendence was held as the preserve of priests and mystics, and portrayed as world-denying, it could enslave people by keeping them beholden to an ideal they would never attain. He thought that empathy could become a way of avoiding yourself by projecting your own troubles onto others: anyone who has suffered the claustrophobic pity of a person who regards themselves as "deeply caring" can appreciate the bad faith of that. Nietzsche's approach was complex and often violent as he sought to throw off these aberrations of true feeling, but it was not simply to dismiss the possibility of transcendence or the value of empathy rightly construed. For example, in *The Gay Science*, he talks about how people routinely abuse the notion of love. They use its unimpeachable status in the hierarchy of virtues as a smokescreen for an avarice that would actually possess the beloved, keep them only for themselves, have them and hold them in a pejorative sense. But, continues Nietzsche:

> Here and there on earth we may encounter a kind of continuation of love in which this possessive craving of two people for each other gives way to a new desire for lust for possession – a *shared* higher thirst for an ideal above them. But who knows such love? Who has experienced it? Its right name is *friendship*. (1974: §14)

Another post-Enlightenment approach reinvents transcendence in a different way. It was behind Mill's thoughts on the value of committing to ends in themselves. The meaning of such pursuits stems from the way they too seem to stand apart from us, while remaining within the sphere of the human. They can be reached out and connected to in committing to an interest, an idea or an understanding of the world.

The contemporary philosopher Peter Singer falls in this camp. In his *How are We to Live?* he reflects on what he calls a "transcendent cause". It is a principle that reaches beyond your own private concerns, the individual submitting instead to something that is part of history or an "evolution of consciousness". Ideally it is an ethical commitment. For while people can give themselves to a wide variety of causes and find fulfilment in them – from football teams, to commercial organizations, to political parties – when they are ethically focused, focused on instantiating the good in life, the cause finds a firmer foundation for meaningfulness and is resistant to the trivial, sectarian or selfish.

Singer's own transcendent causes have been a commitment to animal liberation and care for the environment. At one level, they matter to him personally in the sense that if, say, the planet warmed up too much it would detrimentally affect his quality of life. But that is not the primary reason for his being involved; he has moved beyond an instrumental concern. The weightier matter is that millions of others might die as a result of environmental disaster, countless species of living organism would be wiped out, and the planet itself would be marred. Such a commitment seems necessary to him to be fully human, and so is a fundamental part of his wellbeing. Singer writes of:

the need for commitment to a cause larger than the self, if we are to find genuine self-esteem, and to be all we can be. In sharp contrast to [the] idea that any activity is as good as any other, as long as it is what we want to do, this suggests that some causes are more suitable than others for putting meaning into our lives. (1997: 253)

A third form of exclusive humanism that responds to this aspect of wellbeing can be found in relation to science. Strictly speaking "science does not think", as the philosopher Martin Heidegger put it (1972), which is to say that its reductionist methods are indifferent to meaning and values. However, for some scientists, at least, the draw their discipline has for them rests firmly on the transcendent response it evokes in them.

The writer Douglas Hofstadter is one. He has described how the reductionism inherent in science doesn't produce in him the instinctive revulsion that important things are being "explained away" that he has noticed in others, often of a religious disposition. Rather, it is that very reductionism that brings to him a naturalistic sense of the transcendent:

> I don't know why some people have this horror whilst others, like me, find in reductionism the ultimate religion. Perhaps my lifelong training in physics and science in general has given me a deep awe at seeing how the most substantial and familiar objects or experiences fades away, as one approaches the infinitesimal scale, into an eerily insubstantial ether, a myriad of ephemeral swirling vortices of nearly incomprehensible mathematical activity. This in me evokes a cosmic awe. (1980: 434)

I can see what Hofstadter means. Take the apparent fine-tuning of the constants of the universe (Davies 2006: ch. 8), the values of certain fundamental features of the universe that are right for life to an extraordinarily high degree. For example, so-called dark energy is balanced to one part in 10 to the power of 120, or thereabout. This is equivalent to the probability of tossing a coin and getting 400 heads in a row. And just how unlikely that is can be indicated by saying that if all the atoms in the known universe were coins, and each was flipped a billion times a second, the age of the universe today might just about have allowed one atom/coin to have produced 360 in a row by now. Fine-tuning is just one example of scientific reductionism that yields wonder: an amazement at existence itself that is captured in an astonishing statistic.

Having said that, I also understand the fear that people have at science's reductionist methods. The advantage of squeezing something into a test tube is that it can be scrutinized and measured. But like examining happiness through the lens of pleasure, and coming up with instrumental results, the worry is over what gets left out or distorted. And that might be the central issue, although it is effectively discarded perhaps for little better reason than that the scientific method fails to grasp it.

Theists and agnostics

These are immanent possibilities for some sense of transcendence. They differ from the traditional sense of transcendence that the Enlightenment called into question, since they cut out the theistic dimension. However, that did not result in an end to the belief that human wellbeing depends on God. Even a cursory survey of faith in the modern world suggests that, if anything, such an idea of happiness is resurgent. It is striking too that many of the strongest strands in religion are precisely those that stress the benefits for the individual, Christian evangelicalism being a case in point, with its concern for a personal relationship with Jesus and that being an experience of joy.

In the Christian tradition, the transcendent is resolutely connected to another world, the "City of God" in Augustine's phrase. God makes for human wellbeing by putting His transcendence to one side, descending into the immanence of this world and, through love and sacrifice, redeeming humankind so that believers may rise to eternity in glory. It is transcendence explicitly couched in the doctrinal language of a particular faith tradition. It is religious experience that reflects the narratives of the larger theological system, and finds its summation in the affirmation of a creed. The Anglican bishop Hugh Montefiore provides an example of such a case in his autobiography.

> I was, as I remember, indulging in a rather pleasant adolescent gloom. I suddenly became aware of a figure in white whom I saw clearly in my mind's eye. I use this expression because I am pretty sure that a photograph would have showed nothing special on it. I heard the words "Follow me". Instinctively I knew that this was Jesus, heavens knows how: I knew nothing about him ... I found that I had become a Christian as a result of a totally unexpected and most unusual spiritual experience, although that was not how I would have put it at the time.
>
> (1995: 1)

For Montefiore his experience only made complete sense when it was shaped by a particular belief system and interpreted as carrying implications for a doctrinally committed faith.

I have said that I write as an agnostic. I remain open to the possibility of God, although do not find it helpful to commit to a particular religion. In its doctrinal details, Christianity, in particular, the faith that I know best, just seems implausible to me. On the other hand, I find it hard to see how an exclusive humanist approach – one that insists that everything is ultimately this-worldly, transparent, describable – can be humanly satisfying. To my mind, such a stance deepens, not resolves, the crisis for human wellbeing: only some sense of higher flourishing has the capacity to raise the human sphere to significance, and transform the flat, emptiness of the otherwise ordinary.

So I seek a "middle way": another approach to the transcendent in between the exclusive humanist and the doctrinally religious. It is non-theistic, agnostic, content to rest with certain uncertainties.

Apparently the Buddha refused to answer the question of whether he thought God exists because he considered it to be a distraction from the business that counts, namely, the practical matter of enlightenment. For those who agree, God is simply the wrong place to start, and it is not the place we are at. To insist first on God would be like standing at the foot of a mountain whose peak, locals said, was perpetually covered in cloud, and insisting that you wait until the skies clear and the summit is seen before beginning the climb. Rather, agnostics are like astronomers, for whom the distant universe only takes shape once they have learnt how to see by the elegant means of mathematics and telescopes, which in turn reveal deeper unknowns. Or there is the little girl, remembered by Graham Wallas in his book *The Art of Thought*, who "being told to be sure of her meaning before she spoke, said, 'How can I know what I think till I see what I say?'" We seek a third way: resting on neither God denial nor affirmation.

What is the case, though, is that the transcendent is moral in character; it has to do with the good in life because it has to do with what appears as supremely good. The difference here can be denoted by thinking about numbers. Numbers are transcendent too, in that they exist outside space, time and the world of physical things. But doing mathematics is not usually thought of as a moral activity, the difference being that numbers have no moral quality. Spiritual transcendence, by contrast, is a desire for the good and meaning that underpin wellbeing.

Philosophical charism

The middle way that I am advocating can manifest itself in a number of contexts. For one thing, it is an appreciation of the transcendent that might be gained through the exercise of reason and the mind. It may be a kind of rational intuition that emerges as philosophical arguments are rigorously pursued to their conclusions; it brings about illumination of a logical rather than experiential kind, although in fact the distinction is not readily maintained – one melds into the other. With that melding comes about a radical reorientation of the way the world is perceived, and one that lasts.

I believe that such a yearning for transcendence actually reaches back across the philosophical tradition to its earliest days. One interpretation of Zeno, the pre-Socratic philosopher, is to see his famous paradoxes as pressing at the limits of cognitive thought in order to gain glimpses of what his teacher Parmenides gnomically referred to as "what is". Consider the one in which Zeno confounds common sense by arguing that in order to get from A to B you must first travel half the distance between A and B, and then half the distance between the halfway point and B, and then half the distance between the three-quarters-way point and B, and so on: always halving the distance and so apparently never quite arriving at B. The thought experiment might be taken simply as rationally exposing the paradoxes of infinity: showing that there are an infinite number of discrete moves you could make between A and B in order to travel the finite distance between A and B. However, another way of treating the thought experiment is to see it as a kind of experience of the limits of reason. Under this reading, Zeno intends to lead his readers to the threshold of a deeper appreciation of reality that can be indicated by deductive argument, but not captured by it. At that moment it opens up a new experience of consciousness that is somehow beyond human comprehension. It is transcendent.

As Parmenides, put it, "in the beliefs of mortals there is no true trust": somehow pushing through to a place where truth can be trusted might be called the original charism of philosophy. With Parmenides, writes Raymond Tallis, "thought and knowledge encounter themselves head on for the first time ... such a huge advance in self-consciousness that it is no exaggeration to call it an 'awakening'" (2008), thoughts Tallis explores fully in *The Enduring Significance of Parmenides: Unthinkable Thought*. What Parmenides is after is finally going to be intuited only as an experience of transcendent being, not as a cognitive proposition: reason is the means not the end. It is striking, for example, to compare the description of higher states of meditative consciousness, what Buddhists call the *jhanas*, and the kind of conceptions to which Parmenides appeared to be pointing. "One-pointedness" is one of the key phrases, as is consciousness of objectless, infinite space and, finally, perception merging with non-perception. As far as I can understand it, this is to talk of being itself, through the dichotomies of subject and object, one and many.

Existential spirituality, as discussed say by Jaspers, is a contemporary tradition that inherits this route to the transcendent. In his book, *Way To Wisdom: An Introduction to Philosophy*, Jaspers describes the philosophical task as being to appreciate the subject–object divide through which we, as subjects, perceive the world, as an object. In as much as it is possible to see through this dichotomy, and that possibility is always framed by limited human capacities, the philosopher intimates at being-itself. That is the transcendent. Hence, Jaspers says, the proper name for the meaning of philosophy is mysticism.

For thousands of years philosophers in China, India, and the West have given utterance to a thought which is everywhere and at all times the same, though diverse in its expression: man can transcend the subject–object dichotomy and achieve a total union of subject and object, in which all objectiveness vanishes and the I is extinguished. Then authentic being opens up to us, leaving behind it as we awaken from our trance a consciousness of profound and inexhaustible meaning.

(2003: 33)

For Jaspers, God is the name that signifies such authentic being, as captured by the proposition "God is". "Instead of the knowledge of God," he continues, "which is unattainable, we gain through philosophy a Comprehensive consciousness of God" (*ibid.*).

Deists are other modern inheritors of a similar spiritual rationalism. They gained perceptions of a transcendent principle of reason and order that had wonderfully made the world, with all its laws, intricacies and balance. Today, a number of scientific puzzles commonly emerge as key to the adoption of such a transcendent viewpoint in those who are susceptible to it: how did the laws of nature come to be; how did living mind come to be from lifeless matter; how did the universe come into existence? Science alone cannot answer these questions since it proceeds by formulating laws; the sense of transcendence is precipitated by asking the deeper question of how the principle of law itself originated. At a rational level, this represents an impasse. However, at a spiritual level, an intimation of infinite intelligence, or the universe as an expression of what might be called the mind of God, makes sense. There is something of this, for example, in the insights of Einstein:

> My religiosity consists of a humble admiration of the infinitely superior spirit who reveals himself in the slight details we are able to perceive with our frail and feeble minds. That deeply emotional conviction of the presence of a superior reasoning power, which is revealed in the incomprehensible universe, forms my idea of God. (1927)

Experience and mindfulness

Another way of exploring the transcendent has to do with what might be called religious experience. In his groundbreaking book on these matters, *The Varieties of Religious Experience*, William

James refers to what he calls "cosmic consciousness". It is what one day burst into the life of Canadian psychiatrist R. M. Bucke. As James records, Bucke had enjoyed an evening discussing poetry and philosophy with friends. What happened next is worth quoting at some length for the details his report contains:

> I was in a state of quiet, almost passive enjoyment, not actually thinking, but letting ideas, images and emotions flow of themselves, as it were, through my mind. All at once, without warning of any kind, I found myself wrapped in a flame-coloured cloud. For an instant I thought of fire, an immense conflagration somewhere close by in that great city; the next, I knew that the first was within myself. Directly afterward there came upon me a sense of exultation, of immense joyousness accompanied or immediately followed by an intellectual illumination impossible to describe. Among other things, I did not merely come to believe, but I saw that the universe is not composed of dead matter, but is, on the contrary, a living Presence; I became conscious in myself of eternal life. It was not a conviction that I would have eternal life, but a consciousness that I possessed eternal life then; I saw that all men are immortal; that the cosmic order is such that without any peradventure all things work together for the good of each and all; that the foundation principle of the world, of all the worlds, is what we call love, and that the happiness of each and all is in the long run absolutely certain. The vision lasted a few seconds and was gone; but the memory of it and the sense of the reality of what it taught has remained during the quarter of a century which has since elapsed. I knew that what the vision showed was true. I had attained to a point of view from which I saw that it must be true. That view, that conviction, I may say that consciousness, has never, even during periods of the deepest depression, been lost. (James 1982: 399)

This kind of experience has no doctrinal or faith content, although it does have a distinctive pattern. There is an initial state of detachment, followed by a sudden eruption of the extraordinary. This shock gives way to the world being viewed holistically and as if from outside, with a profound conviction that it is good. The experience itself is relatively fleeting although its impact is long-lasting. It does not result in any prolonged feeling of happiness, but instead an ability to hold on to the convictions felt during the experience regardless of whatever life may subsequently throw up. It yields meaning. James concludes that such experiences carry an immediate authority for those who have them, although not for those who do not. This is because their value does not lie in what they explain, which is nothing, rationally speaking. Rather, it is what they show to the individual concerned that is so transforming, and that may be felt and expressed in any manner of ways. Again, there is the central characteristic of revealing, and revealing something about wellbeing.

Clearly such experiences are very important to those individuals who have them. They do nothing less than colour their sense of existence with an intimation that the ultimately real is good, although beyond the scope of human concepts. But it might be objected that such spiritual experiences, and the sense of transcendent wellbeing they provide, is all well and good for those who have them. But most people do not. If the implication is that you need to be a mystic to have a grounded sense of the good, then surely that puts wellbeing off limits for most.

That, though, is not the conclusion I want to draw. For the extraordinary only matters because of how it yields an insight into the ordinary. In the moment of experiencing the extraordinary a more profound truth of things shows through: that is its value. Wellbeing is to have an appreciation of the transcendent all day, every day. A sense of this might start with a religious experience; it might happen as a result of studying nature, as for Einstein; or even philosophy, as for Zeno. And it might also find a focus through what can be called spiritual exercises.

One obvious example is Buddhist meditation, or, as Buddhists often call it, the practice of mindfulness. Although these spiritual exercises have originated within a religious tradition, they can be practised by anyone and apart from doctrinal commitments. The philosopher of religion John Hick has practised this mindfulness. His analysis in *The New Frontier of Religion and Science* of what it has opened up for him is informative.

He describes how it begins with finding a time, preferably early in the day, before the day's clutter becomes intrusive. As he has been taught by the scholar and monk Nyanaponika Thera, Hick attends to his breathing and watches his mind wandering. Persisting with this first stage produces a second, which happens suddenly, "in which there is no more wandering, consciousness is fixed effortlessly on the breathing alone, and you feel as though you could go on indefinitely, and so go on longer than usual". It is as if your mind is "no longer interrupted", he adds, by the crowd of voices in your head. He continues:

> And just once for me, so far, I have reached a third point. When after being in that second stage for some time I opened my eyes, everything was different, in two ways. Instead of I being here and the room around me and the garden seen through the window there, I was part of one indivisible whole; and, more importantly, that whole, not limited to what I could see, the totality of all reality, was "good", "friendly", "benign", and so that there could not possibly be anything to be anxious or afraid of. (2006: 188)

Hick was not aware of any personal God during this experience, hence putting the words good, friendly and benign in inverted commas. The "good" was as in having a good day; the "friendly" as in user-friendly; "benign" as in benign climate. The occurrence also lasted a very short time although it left an indelible impression. He suggests that Buddhist masters, and those who are able to practise a profound contemplation, are people who have this sense of a good, friendly and benign universe all the time throughout their simultaneously ordinary daily lives.

It is this kind of practice that makes the best sense of the transcendent to me although, like Hick, I could only claim to have had any kind of experience that might count as extraordinary "in the ordinary" on the rarest of occasions. I was once on a retreat that involved practising a form of mindfulness sometimes called *sadhana*. Every day, I would take a walk through a wooded copse near the retreat house that, at a usual pace, would last only five minutes. Then I had to repeat the walk, only this time so that it extended over a whole hour. At first, the experience was rather forced: I attended in studious detail to the shape of a leaf, the crawling of an insect and the pattern of light. But like Hick's experience of his mind ceasing to wander, over the course of the retreat I became less self-conscious and, as each walk began, could become quite quickly aware simply that the copse was a wonderful place to be. Then one day something happened that actually gave me quite a fright. I suddenly felt not that I was looking at the copse, but that somehow the copse was looking at me. It was as if the world turned inside out. It was not me appreciating this small corner of the living world, but the world as a whole was observing me. I presumed I was the subject but had become the object. That was what gave me a fright and I can't say I understand it, although on reflection and in my remembrance the lasting impression is one of a connection that is good.

Some time later I read a book about religious icons, *Lost Icons*, by Rowan Williams. It explained that the point is not so much to look at icons: after all, the saints they depict wouldn't have looked remotely like the image. Rather, the trick is to develop the ability to see figures who are actually looking at you. The gaze of the saint always stares directly out at you. If you dare, you let yourself be seen. That resonates with my glimpses of what I take to be the transcendent.

Discerning mystery

I have dwelt on the experiential appreciation of the transcendent because some kind of existential practice is more important for wellbeing than intellectual understanding, for all that it matters too. To be able to live meaningfully is what Aristotle called practical intelligence; theoretical intelligence is not to live meaningfully but is to talk about what it would be to do so – as we risk only doing here. When ethics is reduced to a purely theoretical matter, as when, say, it is thought to be only about determining rules or principles, it therefore fails. Practical intelligence not only judges well what is a good thing to do, but also, crucially, springs from who you are and what is most becoming of your wellbeing. It involves not only reason and intellect but character, imagination, stories and wisdom; in short, the whole of life's experience.

Kierkegaard has a parable that conveys this:

> Let us imagine a pilot, and assume that he had passed every examination with distinction, but that he had not as yet been at sea. Imagine him in a storm; he knows everything he ought to do, but he has not known before how terror grips the seafarer when the stars are lost in the blackness of night; he has not known the sense of impotence that comes when the pilot sees the wheel in his hand become a plaything for the waves; he has not known how the blood rushes to the head when one tries to make calculations at such a moment; in short, he has had no conception of the change that takes place in the knower when he has to apply his knowledge.   (1978: 38)

This is only to say what any good self-help book would: that reading the book won't help, it is putting into practice what it suggests that might. Peter Singer would say the same about commitment to the causes that he places at the heart of wellbeing: what kind of commitment is it that makes no difference in life? Practice may or may not make perfect but you have to practice nonetheless. It is undoubtedly the case that any kind of insight remains as much ink on the page, or sound in the air if it were spoken, while it is separated from a way of life, while it is not tried out.

However, the intellect counts! For one thing, in the modern world, people can exercise choice when it comes to pursuing wellbeing. In theistic theologies, transcendence ultimately implies a conscious existence outside the natural world, which believers refer to as God. In non-theistic systems, ultimate reality is not thought of as a thing, let alone a person. Brahman, for example, is ineffable, formless, undesignated. In philosophy, transcendence means something else again: the existence of the world that lies behind or through our immediate experience. For better or worse, today everyone must face the question of what they feel they can best commit to, given that they are interested at all. Choice can be confusing and thinking through various possibilities eases the burden.

What gathers the broadly spiritual approaches together is the implication that the foundations of human life – life in the sense of Aristotle's *bios*, or wellbeing as we have defined it – is found beyond humdrum life, even when that humdrum life is pretty good. To put it another way, of all the many things in which an ordinarily flourishing life might consist – friends and freedoms, pleasures and pursuits – transcendence is a special case. The key thing about transcendence is not that it is one more thing in life, even when compared to other things that might be thought spiritual such as an appreciation of beauty, a sense of gratitude, a useful purpose, a love of life. It is not just an element in a life, it colours the whole of life; it is not just the uplifting side of life, but forms the very air that the well-lived life breaths.

Compassion offensive

I think that this is nowhere more clearly seen than in the ethos that, ideally, it inculcates. It can be summed up in a word: selflessness. That selflessness should be part of transcendence stems from its quality of reaching out, to friends and then further. The world can then come to be seen from a wider, global, even God-like perspective. To borrow a term from postmodern philosophy, it is to "decentre" the self, the individual no longer being at the centre of things. Some have said that the revival of such philosophy in recent times was powered by the unforgettable image of the earth rising over the moon, earthrise, as photographed by the astronauts on Apollo 8 in 1968. Human self-centredness is humbled, even mocked, on recognizing the true place our raindrop home has in the black ocean of the universe. It was such a shocking, dislodging experience because the planet directly, and our lives indirectly, were seen as a whole.

Such selflessness differs in tone from the stern moral injunction not to be selfish. I think it is better to think of selflessness as a kind of caring. It is the caring that acts selflessly for another person, as in the justificatory cry, "Why? Because I care about him!" Or it is the "care that killed the cat", as the proverb has it, because the cat's selfless curiosity made her forget her own safety. Robert Pirsig caught something of this kind of selfless caring in another way that relates back to the practice of mindfulness. In *Zen and the Art of Motorcycle Maintenance* he writes:

Zen Buddhists talk about "just sitting", a meditative practice in which the idea of a duality of self and object does not dominate one's consciousness. What I'm talking about here in motorcycle maintenance is "just fixing", in which the idea of a duality of self and object doesn't dominate one's consciousness. When one isn't dominated by feelings of separateness from what he's working on, then one can be said to "care" about what he's doing. That is what caring really is, a feeling of identification with what one's doing. When one has this feeling then he also sees the inverse side of caring, Quality itself. (1974: 290)

The opposite of selflessness, then, would not exactly be selfishness but carelessness. This is because selflessness ultimately stems not from any moral priggishness but from the ancient doctrine of compassion, the practice of empathy. It is so common to religion and philosophy that it is called the Golden Rule.

The ancient Greek playwrights cultivated one form of it in the writing of tragedy, plays that moved the Athenians to identify with the lives of others even when they were their sworn enemies. Alternatively, it is graphically expressed in the Bible in the first letter of John: "But whoso hath this world's good, and seeth his brother have need, and shutteth up his bowels of compassion from him, how dwelleth the love of God in him?" (1 John 3:17). You can find a powerful assertion of selflessness in the caring ethics of Singer too, although I think there is a need to be careful about the reciprocal altruism of evolutionary psychology where selfishness re-enters, as it were, through the backdoor.

The links between selflessness, compassion and transcendence are also clearly explored in Buddhism. It was so from the earliest moments after the religion's inception. Perhaps within days of achieving enlightenment, Siddhāttha Gotama, now the Buddha, made his way back to five of his former companions. According to tradition, he first preached to them about the Eightfold Path and the Four Noble Truths, the core of Buddhist teaching. Then, a few days later, he preached his second sermon. In this discourse he taught them about *anattā*, or the doctrine that a unified sense of self is a delusion. He had examined the various parts of what people think of as making up their self – their bodies, their feelings, their perceptions, their will, their consciousness – and found that none of these components could capture what it was to be an individual. As Karen Armstrong reports in *Buddha*, he concluded: "This is not mine; this is not what I really am; this is not my self". Armstrong continues:

> The human personality is not a static being to which things happened. Put under the microscope of yogic analysis, each person was a process. The Buddha liked to use such metaphors as a blazing fire or a rushing stream to describe the personality; it had some kind of identity, but was never the same from one moment to another. At each second, a fire was different; it had consumed and re-created itself; just as people did. (2000: 101)

Like the Golden Rule, the Buddha's insight is not unique in the history of ideas, although it is rarely as clearly delineated. As dissimilar a person to the Buddha as the eighteenth-century Scottish philosopher David Hume thought similarly. In *A Treatise of Human Nature* he concluded:

> There are some philosophers who imagine we are every moment intimately conscious of what we call our self ... For my part, when I enter most intimately into what I call *myself*, I always stumble on some particular perception or other, of heat or cold, light or shade, love or hatred, pain or pleasure. I can never catch *myself* at any time without a perception, and never can observe anything but the perception. (1960: 252)

Nonetheless, there is a crucial difference between Hume's understanding and that of the Buddha. For Hume, his self-reflection did not necessitate a change in his consciousness of life. He thought that the "bundle or collection of different perceptions" were related to one another, for all that they could not be straightforwardly identified as himself. He concluded that this linking takes place in the imagination; the mind is where the individual is forged. And his perception of the world continued much as it did before he had his temporary identity crisis. Thus, he famously wrote about what he was in the habit of doing after a particularly deep bout of "self searching":

> I dine, I play a game of backgammon, I converse, and am merry with my friends; and when after three or four hours amusement, I wou'd return to these speculations, they appear so cold, and strain'd, and ridiculous, that I cannot find in my heart to enter into them any farther.   (*Ibid.*: 269)

The Buddha's response to uncertainty, like Socrates', was to move in precisely the opposite direction. For him, the sense that the self is ephemeral was not just an intellectual problem, it was a call to transform his way of life, to behave as if he had lost himself. And a strange thing happened when he did. The result was not the collapse of his sense that life was worth living, as Hume perhaps unconsciously feared when he left the disturbing implications of his study for the comforts of the dining room. It did not precipitate a meaningless, unhappy struggle. Instead, in stepping out of himself – the original sense of the word *ekstasis* or ecstasy – the Buddha not only discovered a tremendous sympathy for his companions and the world around him, but in so doing he found transcendence. Compassion, it turned out, was integral to the enlightened state. "The chief requirement of the good life, is to live without any image of oneself", as Iris Murdoch, who had a keen interest in Buddhism, wrote in her novel *The Bell*.

The Buddha had been convinced that compassion was a key to wellbeing. When he had first tasted nirvana, he had thought that he would retreat from public life. Now, though, he was sure that reaching out to others was what it was to be enlightened. It made sense to the Buddha's companions too. For on hearing the second sermon they themselves attained enlightenment: they experienced the ecstasy of what it was to be selfless. Thus the Buddha spent the remaining forty-five years of his life in what Armstrong calls a "compassion offensive".

4. Discerning the mystery

Whatever touch we kindle, and whatever space it may illumi-
nate, our horizon will always remain encircled by the depth
of night.

(Schopenhauer, *The World as Will and Representation*)

Where have we got to in this puzzle with the paradoxes of happiness, the fundamentals of wellbeing, and the search for the good
in life? Well, first, it just seems unskilful to focus on pleasure, no
matter how its positivity is construed. Science needs it, like a train
needs tracks, because it provides something for experiments to get
a grip on. But as happiness is more than mood swings, life is more
complex. Moreover, not only is it impossible to feel good all the time,
it is not good to do so. A smile may be universal but a perpetual
smile is a sign of delusion, or a facelift. Pain is not just inevitable, it
contributes to the good life. Notwithstanding the obvious excep-
tions, suffering is human and can be humanizing. It is necessary
to face that not sideways but head on, and that brought us to the
matter of meaning. Meaning is not only redemptive, it is the crux
of the matter for the human animal. That things have fundamental
significance and undeniable consequence is what puts those things
on the list that people draw up as of the best in life: loving, language,
arts, science, religion. It is natural to say that they are what make
life meaningful, which is to say worth living.

In order to be clear about this, it was my suggestion that
perhaps we should put the word happiness to one side, in favour

of wellbeing. It's not a ban, as indeed I've no desire to be down on pleasure *per se*. Rather, the suggestion is that the word has become a distraction by losing its wider, objective, moral connotations – its link with the good – as resonates, say, through Aristotle's word *eudaimonia*. He sought a life lived well: well-being. And, here's a secret, if you give up on the pursuit of happiness-as-pleasure, although difficult, you find that good feelings still come only they are deeper, more subtle and so more profoundly satisfying. In fact, as was the case with the example of flow, it comes to seem that talking about wellbeing in relation to pleasure or pain misses the point. It is more a matter of contemplation, or passion, or dedication to what has intrinsic value. A focus on that draws closer to the nub of the matter.

Closer still is, I think, the notion of transcendence: that which draws us out of ourselves and enables us to touch something that is not just larger than ourselves but perhaps wholly other, although it is close because it is shown in what is already with us. Spiritual exercises can awaken our attention to this dimension; spiritual experiences, meant in a wide sense, are the apprehension of it. Compassion is the sign and character of this expansiveness, this stepping out of oneself. Such a shift in personal identification, away from the self and towards the other, is so dramatic a change of view that it is called enlightenment. It is to be moral, in the sense of being virtuous, but it is to be more than moral too, for the aim is not to do good but to know what is good by acquaintance. Learning about what is virtuous, Aristotle's intellectual knowledge, is therefore a preparation. Practising what is virtuous cultivates Aristotle's practical intelligence. With that come the goods of life – friendship and family, fudge cake and cappuccinos – and they are good because they are manifestations, to greater or lesser degrees, of the good in life. That is why it is possible to both value such things for what they are in themselves, people clearly being of intrinsic worth, more even than the most beautifully designed product, and allow them to awaken in us the possibility of more, if we care to look.

So let us peer again at the window onto the transcendent. Its appeal to wellbeing, as opposed to the more secular approaches, might be summed up by saying that its meaning goes all the way down. The unique selling point of seeing life as underpinned by a deeper reality is that it can address the big question of the meaning of life itself, rather than the secondary questions of the meaning of this or that activity or presence. Thus when I read Singer I do not think he is wrong so much as wonder whether he has said enough. In my understanding a feeling of transcendence is not created by the causes; more often, it is the reason people are driven to the causes to start with, and believe they are worth sacrificing all to. Causes reflect a belief in an underlying goodness for all the ills manifest on the surface. Similarly with Hofstadter, I feel that he is missing out on something when he only looks down, for he might also look up. It's a bit like scientists researching consciousness who appear to forget that there are already countless studies of the matter, conducted over many times and places, in the form of literature, religion and philosophy. If that material agrees on one thing it is that a mystery runs through it, and a fascinating one at that.

Having said that, it is worth adding that there seems to be a wariness of mystery in many contemporary expressions of full-blown faith these days too. To my mind, this is religion, probably with a capital "R", offered as a transparent system of belief, with a God whom you can know better than your brother and who will do you many more personal favours too. The point is that to be such an adherent of a religion might not mean you are religious at all. The difference, I suspect, rests on your attitude to mystery. To rest with and deepen the questions, and not move swiftly to presumed answers in this or that profession or revelation, marks the difference. The former also seems a better strategy if you seek to know from within, not adopt from without. It's a bit like wellbeing and pain: struggles and doubts are not only human but are humanizing.

The story of the eleventh-century scholar of Baghdad, al-Ghazali, illustrates the point. Ghazali was a man of high mark and political repute when he suffered a kind of mid-life crisis. This seemed like bad news: at its worst point he was able to neither speak nor eat. But this profound crisis in Ghazali's life turned out to be arguably its greatest blessing. For instead of seeking to lessen the dip – to recover perhaps by thinking positively, or rededicating himself to his undoubtedly valuable work – Ghazali pursued the wisdom manifest by his distress. It taught him that he was too much with the world; that he was ruled by pride; that the physical symptoms of his crisis were signs of a spiritual, interior emergency.

He embarked on a long journey and developed new disciplines grounded in Sufism. Then he discovered the key that could unlock his downward spiral: the most important thing in life is to have direct experience of the transcendent – a sense and taste for the infinite – because, as the Sufis say, "The one who tastes knows". He then wrote about it in *The Alchemy of Happiness*, in which he encourages readers to transform the vices of their life into virtues. Hence the analogy with alchemy: the key to happiness is to cultivate the most precious form possible from the rough matter of your life. And why should you want to do this? To make possible the contemplation of the mystery that he called God.

In less overtly religious guise, the philosopher David Cooper has helpfully put it this way: mystery provides a measure of life because it is something for life to be answerable to. He continues:

For if there is not – if all measure is provided from within Life, by the practices, projects and conventions that human beings happen to have devised for themselves – there is no preventing the corrosive conviction that nothing we do is, finally, of significance. Had Life gone differently, we would have been doing different things, and how, in the absence of measure, could we think that this would matter? And if it wouldn't matter, how can it matter either that we are doing what we in fact do?   (2003: 139)

It might be thought paradoxical that mystery provides meaning, as opposed to a complete understanding. Is it not natural to think that if life is to have meaning, that meaning should be found in life, not outside it? The reason it might, though, stems from the fact that human understanding is limited, and so the meaning human understanding can provide is inevitably limited too. To be human is to find ways of talking about what you don't know as well as what you do. Perhaps an analogy with music is helpful. In *What to Listen for in Music*, the composer Aaron Copland wrote: "'The whole problem can be stated quite simply by asking, 'Is there a meaning to music?' My answer to that would be, 'Yes.' And 'Can you state in so many words what the meaning is?' My answer to that would be, 'No'".

Socrates was one of the first to articulate this conundrum within which human beings are caught. On the one hand, we are ignorant of many things, particularly when it comes to what might be called the big questions. On the other hand, we can easily become conscious of that ignorance, just by trying to ask the questions. Man is not the measure of all things, although he can partly measure the extent to which he is not the measure. This may happen when the limits of our understanding are exposed, a service that Socrates spent much of his life performing for his fellow Athenians, earning him the nickname of gadfly. "If a little knowledge is dangerous, where is the man who has so much as to be out of danger?", mused T. H. Huxley. Socrates defined human wisdom as an appreciation of the depths of human misunderstanding. The greatest sage is someone with the keenest assessment of this lack, which is to say the keenest sense of the transcendent.

Theologians call this the apophatic, meaning "negative way". It is a way of talking about something that is ultimately not understood, and is never fully understandable. But it is only ultimately unknown: there is much that might be said before the mystery. The apophatic hones the range of possibilities, or shapes what is mysterious, by clarifying what it cannot be. It discerns the mystery. That sounds esoteric. But apophatic theology will be familiar to church-goers. It lies behind such theological words as "immortal", "invisible", "ineffable". They are used in relation to God, not because they say anything positive about God but because they imply that whatever God might be, God is not mortal, not visible, not effable.

In Eastern traditions, too, something similar can be seen. The Tao is that which cannot be spoken about; it is the nature of nature of Nature, or some such formula of the ineffable. But as the principle of everything, Taoists believe it is the measure.

Another parable by Kierkegaard is illuminating:

When a Greek philosopher was asked to define religion, he asked for time to prepare an answer; when the agreed period had elapsed, he asked for another postponement, and so on. In this way he wished to express symbolically that he regarded the question as unanswerable.   (1978: 74)

And letting the question hang unanswered for so long is not to come nearer to the definition of religion either, Kierkegaard adds!

Theologians say that any talk of God is strictly metaphorical. That is not to say that theology is wrong, any more than that myths are just false stories. It is to say that God-talk is always incomplete and ultimately inadequate. "We know how to talk about God, not because of any understanding of God, but because of what we know about his creatures", wrote McCabe (quoted in Davies 1993: 41).

The same could be said about transcendence: it is possible to talk about it because we know about ourselves and, in particular, our search for wellbeing.

For this way is not proof-seeking, it is sense-making. Reason is important although not as the final arbiter; rather, it is a means of preparation, discernment and interpretation. Questions will remain, of course. What is articulated will, at best, serve only as a guide; there is no absolute clarity to be had, although that could be less of an obstacle than you might think. For as Nietzsche observed in *The Gay Science*, the modern desire for "intellectual cleanliness" when it comes to the veracity of the transcendent, does not feed the human spirit. It ossifies metaphysical systems. It entirely misunderstands the primary motivation for seeking transcendence, namely, that it resonates with a wonder at existence, and an intimation of fundamental goodness. "Whence this new life?", say, in relation to having children; or "Whence this human goodness?", for the charity worker involved in an otherwise hopeless situation. It is not for nothing that both new life and human kindness are routinely referred to as miraculous. They appear to come *ex nihilo*, which is part of saying that goodness and existence are not just part of human life but are possibilities on which human wellbeing rests. The goal of exploring the transcendent is not to unweave these rainbows – to recall Keats's line – but to deepen the intensity of the colours.

It does so by affirming the here and now. "[A]ll shall be well, and all manner of thing shall be well", said Julian of Norwich. Moreover, a clear teaching from most spiritual traditions is that the transcendent, however conceived, should not lead to a withdrawal from this life but should cast it in a different perspective. It is a new awareness not a desire to flee. "Zen ... does not confuse spirituality with thinking about God while one is peeling potatoes. Zen spirituality is just to peel the potatoes", wrote Alan Watts in *The Way of Zen* (1999: 151).

Some more objections

Linking wellbeing with mystery is not a move with which all would agree. What has been said already addresses, I hope, some of the objections that people make – for instance that a turn to the transcendent is this-world denying, or that the advocacy of mystery is an obfuscation, a barely concealed desire to close down the pursuit of knowledge. It is – to continue – different from the kind of connection to which Singer and Hofstadter are alluding. They may be just not that musical when it comes to approaches that smack of the religious, as Max Weber wittily put it: he would gain no more from such an idea of transcendence than a deaf person would from listening to Wagner. It simply passes him by. There are others, like the philosopher Bertrand Russell, who looked at the world and, rather than perceiving any possibility of an underlying unity or goodness, was struck by its divisions and careless indifference. Russell believed that the goodness of humankind is found in precisely the opposite orientation, focusing on the immanent and asserting what human beings and human beings alone can name as good in spite of how things exist in nature, "red in tooth and claw". "For in all things it is well to exalt the dignity of man, by freeing him as far as possible from the tyranny of nonhuman power", Russell writes in "A Free Man's Worship" (1903). If Russell were to recognize that something is lost with the closing of the window on to transcendence, he might describe it as like the loss of childhood innocence: part of growing up. As he put it in *Religion and Science*:

> I believe myself that the assertions [of mysticism] are inessential, and that there is no reason to believe them true. I cannot admit any method of arriving at truth except that of science, but in the realm of the emotions I do not deny the value of the experiences which have given rise to religion. Through

association with false beliefs, they have led to much evil as well as good; freed from this association, it may be hoped that the good alone will remain.   (1997: 189)

He has a point, when you consider the horrors perpetrated in the name of religion. What I am proposing here, though, is that exclusive humanism makes a mistake when it tries to free what it regards as false beliefs from their association with the value of religious experiences. I do not want to try to make a conclusive case for one over the other. Like debates about the existence or not of God, it seems to me that such an approach – thinking of it as a kind of zero sum game – succeeds mostly in turning ever decreasing circles; justifying essentially closed and opposed positions. Instead, carefully noting the objections, not least since they can help hone an appreciation of the transcendent by clarifying what it is not, and lessen the evil that can be associated with mistaken appropriations of it, the question for me is what is at stake for human wellbeing today.

A further point of clarification is perhaps useful at this point; namely, that of the relationship between the human desire for permanence in life and the transcendent, or at least the fear of impermanence. It can be explored by considering the famous story of Leo Tolstoy's religious crisis, which he wrote about in *A Confession*. The novelist recounts growing restless in midlife, oddly enough at the very point when "the two drops of honey" – his love of his family and being a writer – were at their sweetest. You'd think that would be adequate for meaning. It was somehow, though, not enough. "I have seen all the works that are done under the sun; and, behold, all is vanity and vexation of spirit", wrote the writer of Ecclesiastes (1:14). Similarly, life "arrested" for Tolstoy and he had a breakdown: "I felt that all I was standing on had given away" (1987: 32). He could neither understand the meaning of life, nor stop thinking about it. Material science as well as metaphysical speculation did not help. He longed for the transcendent and his agony was only relieved when he stopped trying to answer the question and turned instead to faith. It was faith that enabled him to live. It was faith that showed him what will not be destroyed by death: that which is in union with God.

Now, this experience might be interpreted in a number of ways. An obvious one, perhaps reflecting the assumption that most people would make about the appeal of the transcendent, would be that his crisis had been about the impermanence of life: he'd thought that even his greatest loves – family and work – would not last and so he sought an afterlife of eternity in union with God. However, Tolstoy does not talk about looking forward to life in heaven, or being reunited with his family, so that does not seem quite right. Rather, he is able to affirm that what is supremely valuable now is so not because it will not deteriorate but because it shares in that which is of supreme value: for him, God. Life does not lose its material existence; it gains another dimension of being within that material existence – one that is transcendent. "Something else was also working which I can only call a consciousness of life", he writes (1987: 32). It is rather like Bucke's comment about his cosmic experience: "It was not a conviction that I would have eternal life, but a consciousness that I possessed eternal life then".

Or it is like the thought of a friend of mine, who once told me there was at least a part of him that was content to die because he knew that in his relationship with his partner he loved and had been loved. He had known the good in life. In a way, what more could he want? By the way, the thought did not lead him to contemplate suicide. Instead, the love he knows empowers him to live on all the more.

For Tolstoy peasants showed him this. It is not that they revealed some kind of intellectual knowledge in response to the question of the meaning of life; rather, they showed him how to live and how to live here and now. The philosopher Antony Flew, who wrote an essay on Tolstoy's confession, likened it to some comments of Wittgenstein:

We feel that even if all possible scientific questions be answered, the problems of life have still not been touched at all. Of course there is then no question left, and just this is the answer. The solution of the problem of life is seen in the vanishing of the question. (2000: 216)

Wittgenstein writes elsewhere: "To believe in God means to see that life has a meaning" (1981: 82). It is this seeing what was previously invisible that is the nub of the transcendent affirmation of life. It puts people in touch with fundamental values that go all the way down, thereby providing a sense of ultimate meaning to life. But life is still known as framed by mortality; it is still riddled with impermanence.

The return of transcendence?

People undoubtedly would set other question marks against transcendence. What is striking, though, is that some of the leading writers on wellbeing and happiness today, who would otherwise be signed up as exclusive humanists, are wrestling again with the notion of transcendence in the broadly religious sense. I'm not sure they would put it like this but it is as if they recognize its importance for wellbeing although they struggle with it themselves. Martin Seligman is one, founder of the science of happiness also known as positive psychology and author of *Authentic Happiness*. He refers to transcendence a lot. He argues that there is a whole family of virtues that can be called transcendent, including the appreciation of beauty, gratitude, forgiveness and passion, as well as spirituality, the word he deploys to describe "strong and coherent beliefs about the higher purpose and meaning of the universe" (2003: 156).

In this he is following the evidence, for religion routinely shows up in the research as a positive and powerful force when it comes to people's wellbeing. But there is a question as to whether religion, as in going to church or temple, is the same as spirituality, as in cultivating a perception of transcendence. And then there's Saint Augustine's question, "What do I love when I love God?", which suggests that the essence of religion is not the certainty implied in Seligman's definition of "strong and coherent beliefs". Perhaps it too is designed to be a way of living with uncertainty, discerning the mystery.

That notwithstanding, a scientific link between religion and well-being has been established for some time. It was explored, in the late nineteenth century, by the sociologist Émile Durkheim in a now famous, Europe-wide study of suicide. The one factor that had a greater bearing than all others on the number of people killing them-selves was the constraints that they lived under. It turns out that the greater the obligations people have, the less likely they are to want to end it all. Religion provides the best ties of all. Fyodor Dostoevsky was right: "So long as man remains free he strives for nothing so incessantly and so painfully as to find someone to worship". That which you worship becomes that to which you are tied.

To be more specific, Durkheim argued that it is not religious beliefs *per se* that count. Rather, it is the transcendent connection with other people that religious practice provides that is so valu-able, of which religious conceptions and confessional statements are an expression. Praxis before doxis. "The more numerous and strong these collective states of mind are, the stronger the integra-tion of the religious community, and also the greater its preserv-ative value", he wrote (1970: 170). He believed that religion is a particularly successful way in which people invest their lives with meaning and significance, although, of course, he was not making the instrumental point that it is good to believe in order not to commit suicide!

Alternatively, there is the final chapter in Seligman's book. It is a piece of writing that is almost mystical. He describes how he has never been able to buy the notion of the Judeo-Christian God. Its conception of divinity is just too conflicted for him, necessitating an embrace of the diverse characteristics of creativity, omniscience, omnipotence and goodness that seems to be contradicted by the way the world is. This intellectual stumbling-block is what is often referred to as the problem of evil: why couldn't an all-good, all-powerful, all-wise God design and build a world with less suffering in it? Theologians have composed many responses to this question, if no conclusive answers. Seligman has never been able to swallow their speculations. He has a point.

However, he has read Robert Wright's bestseller *Nonzero*, in which Wright makes the case for evolution having a positive direction. The central observation is that Darwinian forces seem to lead to ever greater complexity in the natural world, having begun by producing single-celled organisms and ended by creating the human brain, an organ so complex that it produces no less a phenomenon than consciousness. But if that is so, then why should the positive achievements of evolution end with consciousness? For one thing, are not human beings moral creatures too? We are awake to the possibility of goodness in the world and seem driven towards that goodness. Seligman speculates that the end point of natural, cultural and cosmic evolution might therefore be a deity who emerges and, at the end of time, comes to know all and is supremely good. On the Edge website, he summarizes it thus:

A process that selects for more complexity is ultimately aimed at nothing less than omniscience, omnipotence, and goodness. Omniscience is, arguably, the literally ultimate end product of science. Omnipotence is, arguably, the literally ultimate end product of technology. Righteousness is, arguably, the literally ultimate end product of positive institutions. So in the very longest run the principle of Nonzero heads toward a God who is not supernatural, but who ultimately acquires omnipotence, omniscience and goodness through the natural progress of Nonzero. Perhaps, just perhaps, God comes at the end. (2007)

He concludes that if to find meaning is to join something that is larger than yourself then, perhaps, by partaking in this process, which will ultimately end in a God who is endowed with omniscience, omnipotence and goodness, people will find meaning.

Seligman's dawning belief, if that is what it is, might be called a new version of deism. It is a notion of divinity that is radically separated from the world as it exists now. The separation is based on the observation that the laws of nature are what govern things, not the arbitrary interventions of a god. However, perhaps paradoxically, the same observation also leads to a new kind of argument for the existence of God by design: the laws of nature "reveal" God in as much as divinity could be the end point to which the natural world progresses by virtue of those natural laws. Similarly, natural laws can be trusted to work for the greater good. In a mysterious way it is on the goodness of the universe that the possibility of your own good life rests. Is this not an attempt to reconnect with the transcendent? Moreover, it would be an appeal to the transcendent that was not just one more thing of which a good life might consist but would underpin the possibility of the good at all.

Spirituality in a scientific frame

Another area of research that appears, perhaps unexpectedly, to be awakening to the possibility of transcendence is neuroscience. Spiritual exercises here have interestingly been called an "off button" for the self. What neuroscience has shown is that during meditation, and in particular the Buddhist practice of mindfulness, the brain's parietal lobes, the parts that help an individual locate where they are in space, become cut off. The lobes are still working: still trying to establish where the individual is and where the boundaries of their physical presence lie. But they don't have enough sensory information to complete the task. The individual, therefore, experiences a dislocation that can be interpreted as losing all sense of self and being part of something vastly larger.

The question is whether the neuroscience is indicating a self-lessness that is genuinely transcendent, or whether it is just a trick of disorientation. Or to recall the spiritual experiences of the previous chapter, might they just be deluded? It depends on how you interpret the evidence, which is to say the worldview you bring to it. For objectively speaking, a case for the former can be made as well as for the latter. I'm inclined to think that this sub-cranial disconnection no doubt happens, along with other activity in the brain. We are psychosomatic creatures. But it is a mistake to see neurons light up and believe that transcendent meaning is dissolving before your eyes and being replaced by an electrochemical event. Meaning is a phenomenon logically associated primarily with the mind, not the brain, although the insubstantial mind is clearly intimately connected to the grey matter. Hick describes the relationship between brain and mind as like that between two dancers: sometimes one leads, sometimes the other. Moreover, consciousness itself, quite as much as spiritual practice, is known to us subjectively. As a physicist might say, they are phenomena that do not possess the property of symmetry: to approach them from the outside in, as science must do, as opposed to the inside out, as we experience them, will always bump up against limitations in understanding. To proceed as if this hurdle doesn't exist is to indulge what Tallis has called "neuromythology". The mind is no more fully understood by describing only what happens in the brain than the aesthetics of a Van Gogh are understood solely by describing his smears of oil paint on the canvas. The smears, like the grey matter, are part of it. The danger is that in making them the main element, as a commitment to science and science alone as a trusted source of knowledge tends to do, the meaningful element is missed out.

The figure of Matthieu Ricard is a fascinating one here. He is a Buddhist monk who trained for over twenty-five years in Tibet and also holds a doctorate in biology. His supervisor was a Nobel laureate. In an effort to bring the two worlds together, Ricard has allowed himself to be studied in a laboratory, his brain being scanned as he practised different kinds of meditation: mindfulness, visualization and compassion. The experiments confirm that meditation is not only a physical phenomenon; brain scans indicate that flow-like states of contemplation are achieved by individuals highly skilled at meditation. For Ricard it also supports what many centuries of Buddhist practice has known: empathically to identify with another person or state of being evokes an intuition that so changes your perspective of the world that it can be called enlightenment. To put it in the language of spiritual practice, the moral person is not just someone who reasons in the right way; it is someone who *is* moral. They are changed. They have become wise, egoism being a form of ignorance because it does not know about other people and states of being. They know in the subjective sense of "I know that feeling so well" as well as the objective sense of "I know the sun will rise tomorrow". They have a new awareness, a perception of wellbeing.

Another individual who I think would fall in the exclusive humanist bracket, but has recognized the importance of studying these matters, is Jonathan Haidt, notably in *The Happiness Hypothesis*. Another positive psychologist, he uses the nineteenth-century novel *Flatland*, by Edwin Abbot, to say why he thinks it matters. Flatland is a two-dimensional place. One day it is visited by inhabitants of the three-dimensional place Spaceland. A sphere from Spaceland tries to explain what it is like to have height, as well as length and width, but the Flatlanders neither understand nor believe it. Then one of the inhabitants of Flatland, a square, has a kind of religious experience. It suddenly sees three-dimensions – what it would be like to be a cube – and consciousness changed by the revelation, struggles to persuade his fellows, although they think him ridiculous. The analogy is clear. Much of modern life is lived in two-dimensions although it can sometimes massively expand into a third. "My research on moral emotions has led me to conclude that the human mind simply does perceive divinity and sacredness, whether or not God exists", he writes (2006: 238), although for Haidt, who is not religious, it does require squeezing spirituality into a scientific frame.

And herein lies a problem. Empirical science is not the natural language of transcendence. It is a little like studying the world in black and white because you don't have a camera that can detect colour. Many things can be understood in monochrome. For example, Haidt explores what he calls the "ethic of divinity", the attitudes that aim to preserve a sense of the "third dimension" in life, such as what anthropologists call purity and pollution. Studies have shown that attitudes of disgust towards certain things, such as certain foods and sexual practices, serve to police boundaries between what is regarded as sacred and profane. This shows up the sacred and makes the transcendent visible in life. The problem for Westerners who have lost these taboos, for very little in the West is now regarded as polluting, can be understood as a collapse of higher flourishing. You can eat pretty much what you like and sleep with pretty much whom you choose. There are undoubtedly many benefits that come with such liberties, not least if you are gay, a menstruating woman, or enjoy bacon sandwiches. However, there is a downside too; namely, a crisis of meaning that comes with a "desacralized", flat culture.

Nonetheless, again, the desire for transcendence lives on. Even the most committed materialist atheist will have, say, places that are special to them, perhaps the place of their birth, or the spot where they first set eyes on their beloved, or the theatre in which they first heard Beethoven's Ninth. For those amenable to religious transcendence, Haidt identifies what he calls periods of elevation, kind of flowful peaks of positive emotion. In a paper entitled "Elevation and the Positive Psychology of Morality", he describes it in this way, recalling some words written by Thomas Jefferson:

> [Jefferson] described the eliciting condition for elevation as the presentation to our "sight or imagination" of any "act of charity or of gratitude". He described the motivational tendency as "a strong desire in ourselves of doing charitable and grateful acts also". He described the affective phenomenology (what it feels like) as feeling "elevated sentiments" and a feeling of moral improvement (feeling oneself to be a "better man"). (2003)

To capture Jefferson's spontaneous acts of charity or altruism, Haidt deploys one of the Greek words for love, *agape*: an overflowing of love in the presence of what is recognized as moving and true. *Agape* might be elicited by an experience of awe, too, such as surges on beholding something wonderful in nature, or imagining something tremendous in the mind. This is an experience of self-transcendence, defined by Haidt as perceiving something vast that cannot be fully grasped by your own mental apparatus.

In this way, Haidt reintroduces an exclusive humanist notion of transcendence into an account of what truly makes for wellbeing. It is what he calls "vital engagement", when something someone is doing or experiencing, perhaps work or love, is in perfect alignment with what they are as a person and where they are in terms of their social and cultural environment. Everything makes sense. Haidt concludes:

> Happiness is not something that you can find, acquire, or achieve directly. You have to get the conditions right and then

wait. Some of those conditions are within you, such as coherence among the parts and levels of your personality. Other conditions require relationships to things beyond you: Just as plants need sun, water and good soil to thrive, people need love, work and a connection to something larger. It is worth striving to get the right relationships between yourself and others, between yourself and your work, and between yourself and something larger than yourself. If you get these relationships right, a sense of purpose and meaning will emerge.

(2006: 238)

And yet, this conclusion demonstrates to me the challenge to the kind of approach to wellbeing that can't embrace a religious account of transcendence, the taste for the infinite that provides meaning because it goes all the way down. For although he follows the evidence, and searches for transcendence, Haidt's account of it, based as it is on the language of science and science alone, inevitably falls short. It stops just at the point when it is getting interesting! He effectively takes the "trans" – from the Latin for "beyond" – out of transcendence.

Not being open to the "possibilities of meaning and of truth that lie outside of empirical seizure or proof", to recall Steiner's phrase, shows itself in a number of very specific problems with the idea of wellbeing that follows on from it. For example, Haidt fails to draw clear distinctions between elevation that is gained through experimenting with drugs and that from spiritual exercises. When the transcendent is basically described as elevated positive emotion how could he? There are, though, many reasons to think that there is a difference. For example, spiritual exercises are designed to open you up to a deeper reality whereas drugs, for the most part, are taken to close reality down, as in being "off your face". Some drugs like LSD have been used in exercises in mind expansion, and credited as catalysts for spiritual and personal growth. And it may well be the case that certain chemicals washing through the brain evoke physiological changes that are similar to those observed when, say, monks are meditating. But drug-taking is a clumsy way of triggering unity and joy, perhaps akin to using a mallet to break eggs for an omelette: at one level it works but it leaves you with a mouthful of shell not fluffy omelette. Or remember Nozick's thought experiment with the happiness machine. People on the whole do not want to be plugged into it, feeling its contentment would be inauthentic. Similarly, few, I imagine, would seriously suggest that a life spent on drugs was ideal. Huxley knew this when he wrote *Brave New World* featuring the drug soma. He describes the experience of taking the soma as "lunar eternity"; it makes everything seem good; it facilitates rapt attention. It seems like transcendence, except that it also turns those who imbibe it into zombies. (Why Huxley resorted to taking mescaline a decade or so later is another question entirely.) Religiously speaking this is because the effects of drug-taking are not a true, but a flawed and ultimately damaging, imitation of spiritual elevation.

Another difficulty stems from the notion of transcendence as peaks of emotion. This understanding draws on the work of the psychologist Abraham Maslow. Maslow is famous for his hierarchy of needs. He placed bodily, animal needs on the lowest rungs of the ladder and spiritual, uniquely human needs at the top. Peak experiences are one way of satisfying such higher needs, according to Maslow, providing a sense of meaning and connection. But while his motives were positive – to invigorate the discipline of psychology by injecting it with a concern for human values and truths – his analysis is problematic. In *Selling Spirituality*, Jeremy Carrette and Richard King analyse why that is, highlighting a number of elements. There are sometimes questions to be asked about the science itself. Alternatively, Maslow came to his analysis with predetermined ideas as to what valid spiritual experience might be, largely determined by phenomena that science could measure and understand.

"Sampling disillusioned college graduates, Maslow would ask his interviewees about their ecstatic and rapturous moments in life, not realizing that religious insight often came from experiences of suffering and denial", explain Carrette and King (2005: 75). His work was predetermined by his values: essentially treating the search for the transcendent as "a cultural sedative providing individual rapture", a kind of super-feel-good experience.

The challenge of the transcendent

There is another problem of working with a reduced conception of transcendence. As Haidt concludes, the key to wellbeing becomes some kind of synthesis, the "from between". In terms of its binary basic structure, this appears to reflect an insight that is as old as the question of happiness itself. Ancient Greek myths included stories about the so-called choice of Hercules: the hero reaching a point in his life when he had to decide either on a life of licentious pleasure or a life of challenging virtue. Being a hero, he opted for the latter, and it brought satisfaction, although only after facing the twelve labours that almost destroyed him.

Alternatively, Aristotle talked of the "Golden Mean", the notion that the virtues that open someone up to *eudaimonia* are located at the mid-point between extremes of human behaviour: courage is neither cowardice nor foolhardiness; modesty is neither shyness nor shamelessness. Or there is his analysis of friendship as a kind of extension of yourself with the friend who is another self: connection is found "from between". A similar merging of opposites comes through in Durkheim's analysis: religion is so marvellous for the people he studied since it provides a sense of belonging to others that is simultaneously a valuing of your own life. If you are left on your own, he suggests, you do not find freedom; rather, you feel lost and possibly suicidal.

But without an adequate understanding of the transcendent, seeking a synthesis of these two aspects turns out to be a fool's game. Ziyad Marar, in *The Happiness Paradox*, has helpfully identified these opposing dynamics as so difficult to unite because within an immanent frame they are actually contradictory. Generalizing, he calls one side of the equation the need to feel free, and the other the need to feel justified. The former is about expressing your individuality; the latter is about admitting your dependency on others. In short, the one requires you to give up at least some aspect of the other.

It seems that it is well-nigh impossible to get this balance right, which offers another reflection on why the advice of the happiness gurus tends not to work in practice. Families, the research shows, deliver happiness because they provide security, until, that is, your family becomes a source of unhappiness and you long to be rid of it. Work is another case in point: a fulfilled day in the office, ideally with some moments of psyche-stretching flow, is profoundly satisfying, until, that is, work becomes mind-numbingly boring and you only stick with it because you have to earn a living. Or take the call to keep fit: going to the gym seems like a win–win situation – it makes you healthy and provides you with an endorphin rush – until, that is, the discipline of working out becomes overbearing and you long for the easy life of those who are fat and happy.

Marar understands this, although his own exclusive humanism leaves him pessimistic about the possibility of long-term wellbeing. He believes the paradoxes of happiness are irresolvable in the modern world because people have lost a sense of the religious dimension within which they might seek a resolution of the opposing pressures in life. Thus Aristotle's Golden Mean was not an end in itself – a balancing act – but was a way of opening yourself up to the third, transcendent dimension that made sense of what the individual was trying to achieve. It is called turning to God in faith traditions, "whose service is perfect freedom", in the words of the old prayer book. Note the paradoxical identification of liberty and justification in that "freeing service".

And there's the clue, for the divine perspective or religious dimension – what I am calling the transcendent – creates a new possibility of freedom that is also a submission. Freedom is not merely the acts of an individual expressing themselves, making any number of choices that could in theory be infinite. After all, bad choices lessen freedom by imprisoning the individual. Rather, freedom is deciding on a specific path in life. If wellbeing, as I am suggesting, is found in choosing a path towards the transcendent because it is that which speaks to us of the good, then freedom is actively pursuing the good, not just in any old acts but in those that develop the character, will and disposition – what Aristotle helpfully called the "intelligent appetite" – to act in accordance with the good. To put it more succinctly, as McCabe does, the free will is one that wants to act well. It knows that the good is supremely desirable and, in seeking it, slowly, unsteadily but surely becomes good too. Needless to say, none of this makes much sense when the transcendent is interpreted merely as elevation. What is missing is a notion of the transcendent good.

Hence the crunch issue for contemporary wellbeing; what I believe is lost when we give up on the possibility of real transcendence is nothing less than the hope of lasting wellbeing. Put more positively, maybe the new science can be thought of not as surpassing the old wisdom but, by becoming conscious of the limits of its empiricism, as actually an invitation to return to it. Transcendence matters because the tensions between freedom and justification, individuality and belonging, pleasure and suffering, cannot be resolved within ourselves, only outside ourselves. In an Enlightenment Flatland, we can turn to other people, and to a rational conception of morality. They are valuable, indispensable. They are good things, but they will tend to let us down, and we them, because we and they do not go all the way down. What we need is different from a jaunty, worldly optimism, although that might help. It is a more profound confidence born of the spiritual.

This conclusion is an awkward one. The sceptics will resist it for the implication that the rational capabilities of humankind are not enough, or because they have no sense and taste for real transcendence, or because they perceive in this talk the search for a consoling eternity with God. They would be right about the limitations of human reason but not about the need for one set or another of metaphysical beliefs, for what transcendence turns on is not divinity but mystery. It is mystery that yields a sense of meaning that counts. It isn't comprehensible, but works for the very reason that it isn't comprehensible. Mystery is not empty either, as again the sceptic might suspect. It is characterized by the act of compassion that, as *ekstasis*, or a stepping out of yourself, is to reorientate yourself towards the transcendent. That is not guaranteed by belief in a god, although for some faith undoubtedly helps. Its prior sense is rather one of infinite wonder at what is good, what is beautiful, what exists.

It is from that selfless, careful perspective that the tensions between freedom and justification find themselves resolving by dissolving, since strictly speaking freedom and justification are concerns of the ego. Obviously, this is no easy matter to achieve. One swallow does not make a spring, as Aristotle reflected: wellbeing is a lifetime's achievement. Our examination of religious experience suggests that for most, all that is possible is a momentary glimpse of such a state of mind. It is the good in life that they taste; a good life remains a constant effort to realize. However, with that glimpse an image of the possibility is imprinted on the mind, like dark mountains at night briefly floodlit by a distance discharge of lightning. With that memory of transcendence all manner of apparent impossibilities become possible.

This is what Ricard hopes the science of happiness will lead people to, as he gently discusses in *Happiness*. Ricard too conceives of enlightenment not as a union with some transcendent object that is beyond reach, but as of this world and beyond our usual conception of it. "The real problem is that it is so close we can't see it, just as the eye doesn't see its own lashes", he writes (2003: 263). While enlightenment is a mystical state in which the divide between subject and object is transcended, "above and beyond the fabrications of the intellect", it is not a transmigration to another world; it is the transformation of now.

It is also not one project among many others, as if it were just one option people might choose as part of their wellbeing, a kind of *à la carte* spiritual exercise. It is the very possibility of lasting wellbeing. "Again, the major shortcoming of the utilitarian system, in the long run, is the risk of confusing pleasure with genuine happiness, or more accurately, of reducing the latter to the former", Ricard continues (*ibid.*: 247). Pleasure matters. Meaning matters more, and the transcendent good underpins it. He concludes by focusing on what is the real goal:

> Enlightenment is what Buddhism calls the state of ultimate freedom that comes with a perfect knowledge of the nature of mind and of the world of phenomena. The traveller has awakened from the sleep of ignorance, and the distortions of the psyche have given way to a correct vision of reality.
>
> (*Ibid.*: 263)

5. The power of love

Our life problem is one of the transformation of energy.
(Iris Murdoch, *Metaphysics as a Guide to Morals*)

The Buddhist vision is just one of the great religious and philosophical traditions that see reality as only properly understood with the
transcendent dimension. It comes through meditation, since it is
wisdom above and through any purely intellectual insight; it is in
but not of the humdrum and everyday. In fact, the body is thought
of as the gateway for such a deeper sensibility – the universal is
found in the particular, to deploy the technical terms – which is
why Buddhist teachers put such store on silence and stillness, "just
sitting". Then you can really notice the movements of mind and
the messages, pleasurable and painful, of the body. Mindfulness
is nurtured in Buddhist training because that prepares the individual for the flashes of non-conceptual intuition and experience
that, with discernment, bring understanding and are the grounds
of wellbeing.

Personally, I think there is much in what is beginning to be
explored in the interaction between Eastern and Western thought.
For instance, there is the possibility that Western philosophy has
almost stalled when it comes to offering a vision of life because it
has become too intellectual – too intellectually brilliant, you might
say – that brilliance casting the need for practical intelligence in
the shade. In all the technical talk between academic philosophers,
conducted almost exclusively among themselves, philosophy has

become stuck on the conceptual. This is Kierkegaard's difference between building a palace and living in a kennel that I referred to in the introduction. It has lost touch with the wisdom that can show people the place where the mystery can be discerned, meaning found and life lived well. As one eminent philosopher once said to me, "I rather doubt that life has a meaning. If I thought perhaps it did, and I wanted to find out what its meaning is, I don't imagine I'd ask someone whose credentials consist of a PhD in philosophy." A witty comment, but a tragic one, for it left me wondering whether it was philosophy that had undone his faith in meaning too.

This spirit, or rather lack of spirit, is perhaps why when contemporary philosophy turns to the question of how to live it can derive robust theories of conduct, rules that aim to deliver good consequences, and coherent rationalizations of what wellbeing might be, but they seem rather flat and dry: a question of calculation and balance, of stamina and will-power. That is important but it is not enough. This would be another result of the wider cultural shifts that, deploying Charles Taylor's distinction, can be noted as a decline in higher flourishing and preoccupation with the lower. But the practice is needed because, again as we noted in the introduction, "Knowledge we could never attain, remaining what we are, may be attainable in consequences of higher powers and a higher life, which we may morally achieve", in the words of William James. To put it another way, a science of life is one thing; the art of living is where it comes to life.

So you could be forgiven for thinking that my final recommendation is become a Buddhist! Not quite. It is still Western philosophy that has brought me to these conclusions or, to be precise, ancient Greek philosophy thought of as the pursuit of a way of life in search of the good in life. That is a synthesis of the intellectual understanding of philosophy as it has come down to us today, human psychology, personal reflection and a religious sensibility. What Aristotle, Plato and others were saying can seem somewhat odd to us today, as in relation to *eudaimonia*, although in large part I think that stems from the modern disconnect. In other words, understanding what they were saying is a challenge. But it is not so distant as to be simply baffling and alien, like, for instance, the philosophy of the ancient Egyptians with its good life attendant on burying kings and mummifying cats.

People still read the Greeks and Romans. Their philosophy as a way of life is intelligible, illuminating. Moreover, it can provide us with a language of transcendence, and wellbeing, that, while having much in common with that of the East, is perhaps more immediate in the West, making us feel more, as it were, at home. I have been using this language already, in the talk of virtue and the good. But if there is one word that stands at the centre of their vision, although as yet I have held it in the wings, it is this word: love. It was particularly important for Plato. So in this final chapter let us turn to him, and see what can be made of it. My hope is that he shows how all that has been said can be knit together, in particular the intellectual with the practical, the skilful thinking with the skilful living: to cut to the chase, what might more helpfully be put as skilful loving. For if it is right that the challenge of the transcendent is the issue on which contemporary wellbeing hangs, that translates into approaching wellbeing not as primarily being about what you will do, or how you will live, or what you will call good or bad, although that will all follow. Rather, it is what you love.

The three-part soul

First, take a step back and ask another question. What is it to be human? Or what are we at heart? What single word, image or myth has an impressive ability to capture the key part of us?

Many possibilities have been toyed with over the centuries. Sophocles implied we are the plaything of the gods, hurled about like lightning, although burning up in tragedy not light. For seventeenth-century mathematician Blaise Pascal we are reeds, "the weakest thing in nature", although redeemed because we are "thinking reeds". Benjamin Franklin picked up on the emerging successes of modern technology, describing a human being as "a tool-making animal" – and nothing short of brilliant in that capacity. Mark Twain injected some tenderness back into our creatureliness, whimsically noting that, "Man is the Only Animal that Blushes. Or needs to". Tragic, thinking, tool-making and/or tender? The truth is that trying to arrive at an indisputable essence of humankind is hard, which is perhaps why some philosophers have denied there is an essence at all.

Plato had an idea, probably original, about the structure of human individuals that proved to be strikingly productive. He thought that any model of our nature needed to be composed of three distinctive yet interoperable parts. A trinity of elements has the capacity to capture what anyone can perceive, even after a modicum of self-reflection: we are divided selves.

That we are divided two-ways is immediately obvious and arises in many contexts. There is the perception, say, that we are divided between mind and body. My mind can tell me to stop smoking, while my body longs for a cigarette. Or my mind can stand aside from the tooth aching in my mouth, while my body is wholly preoccupied with it. Alternatively there could be a two-way division between our rational and emotional capacities. I can sit down and reason that I am up to the task, while my feelings run cold with a sense of inadequacy. Or I can equivocate about what might be the right thing to do, while my feeling is that, yes, I should offer a coin to the beggar on the street.

There are many other such dualities to draw on that fit different situations, from right and left brains, through yin and yang, and reason and emotion, to Dr Jekyll and Mr Hyde. Two-way divisions of the self are pervasive in science, philosophy and literature because they are accurate to a first approximation. To that degree, they add to our knowledge of life. But only to that degree.

For they are perhaps not quite as neat as first meets the eye. For example, the mind depends on the body, not least since the "organ" of the mind, the brain, is part of the body. Alternatively, the body can itself act as if it has a mind, as when, say, someone snatches their hand away from something hot: they feel the pain from the heat afterwards because what causes the motion is the body's automatic reflexes. In other words, like the commentator who has long stopped thinking of football as two teams competing to score goals, a deeper consideration reveals that to reach a lasting settlement on the structure of the self requires more than a bipartisan arrangement.

It is this complexity that Plato's intuition about the value of a tripartite model aims to capture. He pushed the binary reflections a stage further and realized that there is often a third dimension that is active in our confabulations with ourselves. For example, when my mind says stop smoking there is a question here both of whether I have the willpower to say no, and what is best for my health. In this case, the single division of "mind" actually conceals two aspects, one of volition and another of moral choice. It is for this reason that someone can know smoking is bad and never seriously attempt to give up. Alternatively, when I am wondering whether or not to give some money to the beggar, it could be that the emotional imperative I feel is actually the culmination of two separate feelings. One is shame at the miserliness I would feel if I didn't. The other is the sense that whatever the complexities of the situation, justice demands something be done, and so I should not do nothing. This time it is the single division of "emotion" that can be broken down into two parts: a self-regarding gut instinct and a sensibility that has a moral dimension to it.

In the course of his writings, Plato explored various options as to what kind of three-way model works. One of the best appears in what is often referred to as the Great Speech, a discourse that he puts into the mouth of Socrates in his dialogue the *Phaedrus*. Here Socrates likens the human individual to a two-horse chariot driven by a charioteer. The charioteer is perhaps the easiest aspect to grasp. He represents the rational part of the human individual, the element that would take us in the reasonable direction along the course of our lives. Cognitive calculation is certainly part of life but you do not have to be Sigmund Freud to know that it is far from all. We are driven too, often irrationally or at least non-rationally. So in Plato's model the charioteer is not alone. He could hardly be a charioteer if he was. He has two horses that pull him. However, they are not alike, and this is where Plato is able to reflect the sense that life is more complicated than the two-way split allows. For while one of the horses is well-bred, and thus docile and obedient, the other comes from poorer stock and is unpredictable, wild and liable to attempt to break out on its own.

It is obvious what Plato is getting at with the wild horse. This stud is libidinous and as powerful as a stallion. It could as easily throw the charioteer as a night of ill-conceived passion can ruin a marriage. The threat that such erotic madness represents to the individual rises to a peak when he or she comes face to face with another human being of great beauty, which, according to the desideratum of the ancient Greek imagination, was never more powerful than in the goodly image of a statuesque youth. As Socrates describes it in the *Phaedrus*: "[The stud] no longer responds to the whip or the goad of the charioteer; it leaps violently forward and does everything to aggravate its yokemate and its charioteer, trying to make them go up to the boy and suggest to him the pleasures of sex" (254A). It is a familiar feeling. Even Apollo, who was in part a model of sobriety and reason, was overcome at the sight of the beautiful nymph Daphne. He only stopped chasing her because she morphed into a laurel tree.

So much for the stud. What of the third party in Plato's metaphor, that of the second, well-bred horse? What aspect of the human psyche does it represent? According to Socrates, it is as resistant to the lustful shoving of the dark horse as the charioteer, although not out of high-minded reason. Rather, the thoroughbred represents a third part of the human self that is a little less easily defined but, for that reason, goes to the heart of why the model is so illuminating.

This blood-horse stands for what the Greeks called *thumos*. Scholars have spilt moderate amounts of ink discussing just what the word means. Part of the problem is that Plato emphasizes different qualities associated with *thumos* in different places; he also changes its meaning compared with other ancient Greek authors who used the word, notably Homer. Also, there is no direct translation of the word in modern English, although it can be taken as meaning life-force, mettle or moral vigour. Strictly speaking it is an emotional part of the psyche, not rational, differing from brute desire by virtue of being amenable to reason: it thrives on a love of honour and spiritedness, and can be driven by virtuous anger or awestruck fear. It is also the capacity to awaken a sense and taste for the infinite. It is a synthesis of emotional balance and intelligent behaviour, or of vision and action. In a sense *thumos* can be imagined as opening up a third way between the pure lust of the dark horse and the cold reason of the charioteer: where the former is crazy, and the latter calculating, *thumos* is courageous.

Something of this is captured in how Socrates says the thumoeidic horse looks: "His coat is white, his eyes are black, and he is a lover of honour with modesty and self-control; companion to true glory, he needs no whip, and is guided by verbal commands alone" (253D–E). It is the kind of beast that triumphs in all the disciplines of three-day eventing or, in more chivalrous terms, it is the white charger bestrode by a hero who would die for its rider. When it comes to sex, it remains obedient to the charioteer, for all that, as Socrates says, the sight of the youth infuses it with warmth and tingling and the goading of desire; it knows what it is to feel attraction. However, its innate decency helps it maintain control and, "prevents itself from jumping on the boy".

Thumos is the love that will find a way, in contrast to the lust that would have its way. It is the love that begets love, rather than the lust that would exhaust itself in an orgy. It is a kind of intelligent appetite, a love of what is good, whose idea of freedom is to direct all its energy in pursuing it. It is giving and does not count the cost or look for a return; caring not for its happiness but for its virtue – its drawing close to the good. The stud has its part to play, and the charioteer would not want to be uncoupled from it, not least since when in love it can be a source of much fun: "swelling with desire, confused, it hugs the lover and kisses him in delight", Socrates bawdily continues (256A).

However, it is the noble horse that plays a major part in the emergence of any successful relationship. Love may often be ignited by infatuation, but to last and be fulfilling the early passion must become companionate, compassion, selflessly caring and blissful. This is a difficult path for reason alone to direct the individual along because, after the thrills of courting, its wise counsel seems lukewarm at best. This is the perfect metier for *thumos*, though, because it is feeling too. Manifesting itself as passion, although of an amicable kind, it is able to compete with the grasping appetites of lust and suggest the possibility of replacing the pursuit of pleasure with the cultivation of, shall we say, wellbeing.

From lust to transcendence

In terms of relationships, *thumos* generates the emotional courage to drink deeply of the love of another and learn to trust them; it is the courage to be open to a desire beyond mutual gratification. In ethical terms, it describes a quality of relationship that moves beyond the perhaps inevitable selfishness of young love – the love that panics when it does not get its way, that wants to have and exclusively to hold – and raises the possibility of a love that has the capacity for genuine selflessness. It makes the intimacies of commitment and marriage conceivable. Without it, that joyous state of being, soulmateship, would remain below the conceptual horizon.

Moreover, as Plato's account of the course of such friendship continues, another possibility emerges. He says that as love grows, it is as if the chariot teams of the two individuals sprout wings. With that, they find that they are no longer bound to the racing track. Rather, their love lifts them above the terrain of humdrum concerns and their gaze turns outward and heavenward. The awkward self-consciousness of their original attraction could never have conceived of this higher love; it is recognized as being worth more than those earlier, sexy pleasures – it seems inspired by a god, transcendent. "That which is so beautiful and attractive as these relations, must be succeeded and supplanted only by what is more beautiful, and so on for ever", wrote Ralph Waldo Emerson (1841). Bright, free and happy, Socrates says, they travel together as philosophers, which it is helpful to remember translates as "lovers of wisdom", or "higher flourishers". No longer is their love just for each other. It embraces a passion for what is above them both, although they became aware of it only because they found love altogether and their conscious-ness changed, for the good.

Lovers tend to be absorbed in each other, turned face to face, observed C. S. Lewis in *The Four Loves*, also noting that they like nothing better than to talk about their love. Lovers-become-friends, though, might be defined by a transformation of this inwardly directed gaze: they now stand side by side. Love absorbs them but not so much in each other as in their pursuit together of what is true.

Again, what is so striking about this is that Plato suggests it is lovers who come to feel that they can fly. The idea is echoed in a thousand songs, classical and popular, from Richard Strauss's opera *Der Rosenkavalier* with its exquisite trio ending, to Joe Cocker, who wanted love to lift he and his partner "Up Where We Belong" in the song of that name. It is in their sexual desire that their imaginations are opened up to the transcendent. *Eros* can take them higher; and they become even more amazed at the wonder that opens up before them than when they first tasted the happiness of sexual congress. Something is better than sex! There is a realization – how can I put it – that carnal cooling is not a relational calamity. On the other hand, this is not to say that Plato is anti the body, and pro the spiritual, as the phrase "Platonic relationship" might suggest. Nor does his conception of love somehow use human beings as a means to an end, as if he advocated exploiting your lover to awaken in yourself a love for the greater good. This would carry the unappealing corollary that people were not lovable for their own sake, but only in so far as they instantiate the goodness and beauty of higher things. Your wellbeing would then require you to drop former lovers, or dump your partner, after they have served their purpose, enabling you to rise higher, free of that gross thing called the body. Such callousness would seem to be the antithesis of love, and any decent understanding of human wellbeing. It is. Rather, when living life well, all three elements – desire, reason and passion – flourish together. The individual is neither a heartless Lothario nor a sexual psychopath. They are the astonishingly good friend who becomes more, not less, irreplaceable as life deepens, and lust perhaps fades.

Freud's work provides an obvious comparison to make here, he having famously charted a map of psychodynamic life that pits id against ego against superego. The id would seem to correspond to Plato's dark horse; the ego to the charioteer; and the superego to the white steed. However, in Freud there are differences in the third part that are illuminating. For one thing, Freudian psychology would interpret the passion of *thumos* as essentially narcissistic. This is not meant in the pejorative sense, but as the self-respect of *amour-propre*, the concern for ourselves that cares what other people think of us. Plato's conception includes this aspect, notably in the relationship between *thumos* and the ancient Greek virtues of courage and honour. However, he goes beyond a narcissistic interpretation of them to include the transcendent element: that which desires such virtues not only because they make for the wellbeing of the individual, but also because when they are rightly nurtured, the individual is drawn to that which is good for its own sake, the good in life. To put it another way, when contrasted with Freud, Plato's is a positive psychology that attends to the transcendent good not just the higher and lower pleasures.

Another difference of emphasis between Plato and Freud concerns the nature of the superego. Crudely put, Freud portrays the three parts as a predominantly legalistic superego at odds with a libidinous id in a battle royal for which it is the sensitive ego that chiefly suffers. Plato's white horse is similar to the superego in that it understands the force of moral reason, which is why it does not need the whip. However, the white horse is like the black horse in as much as both are fundamentally passionate. So unlike Freud's superego and id, the two horses would seem to have a far greater capacity to work as a team, so long as the charioteer can ensure that they drive forward together. Again, a higher happiness – wellbeing – seems possible in Plato, not merely a transformation of neurotic misery to normal unhappiness, as Freud famously expressed the goals of psychoanalysis (2004: 306).

There is another way in which Plato's idea of love differs from one that commonly does the rounds today, although it might seem similar because they take the same path for a time, and that is romantic love. Romance might be defined as the desire to be lost in love. As it is represented in films, novels and advertisements today, it is captivated by the process of *falling* in love. It is uninterested in the business of *standing* in love, to deploy a distinction made by Erich Fromm (1956).

There is a myth of human origins that explores the difference, told first by the ancient Greek comic Aristophanes, according to

Plato. At first, Aristophanes explains – not without tongue in cheek – humankind existed as three sexes: male, female and hermaphrodite. These aboriginals got a bit above themselves. And as punishment for their hubris, the gods decided to split each in half: the all-males became two men, the all-females two women and the hermaphrodites a man and a woman. The surgery was psychologically traumatic. And ever since human beings have spent their lives looking for their lost halves: heterosexuals to become hermaphrodite wholes once more; homosexuals to return to their all-male or all-female state. Thus, according to the rules of romance, wellbeing consists in finding your "other half".

However, Aristophanes' story doesn't end there. He continued by describing what happens to the lucky individuals who find the one who is out there waiting for them. Naturally, they fall into a lovers' embrace, until they are interrupted *flagrante delicto* by the god Hephaestus. Hephaestus, the patron of craftsmen, has the capability to weld people together, an offer the lovers can't refuse. After all, sexual union is temporary; a pleasure subject to diminution. What lovers long for is to be together forever. And Hephaestus obliges.

The experience is bittersweet. For while the lovers will never be parted, they lose themselves in each other. They are not able to lead very productive lives either. Aristophanes imagines them wrapped in each other's arms, immobile, as if waiting for death. His story turns into a bleak image of love; his comedy is also a tragedy.

What he conveys is somewhat like the plot of romantic literature. At first love thrills but then it kills its lovers. It is Romeo and Juliet, whose first night together is spent in a bed, and second in a sepulchre. Or Jane Austen's sillier subjects, who spend their youth longing for wedlock – with the emphasis on the "lock" – and have no story to tell once hitched because subsequently theirs is the no-life of a loveless marriage. Heavy romance appears to draw you towards a good life, but in identifying the good wholly and exclusively with another human person – demanding that this individual fulfil all your needs – it is unable to make much of transcendent yearning. This is another insight. Human beings desire union; it makes life meaningful. But if that union is sought solely at the level of the human, in another human, then it risks turning in on itself: thus people fall out of love, or become incapable of love, or run out of love. Aristophanes' lovers do not sprout wings and fly; they curl up together and die. They don't know of the expansive love that identifies first with another and then with the Other, the standing in love that finds deep soil into which to sink its roots and grow.

Acknowledging the dangers of loving someone too much is indirectly to draw attention to part of the value of children. Having kids introduces a third person – and perhaps a fourth and fifth – into the relationship. It breaks the deadlock. It draws love out again. Having said that, this is not to advocate the instrumental advice of having children to save a marriage, let alone make you happy. What a friend once told me highlights the difference. She said that she didn't really mind much whether or not she had children until she met her husband and they had married. Only then did the desire to have a family emerge, not as some sense that "the line" should continue or to satisfy a biological urge or to revitalize their relationship, but as an awakening that their love could be shared. It could overflow into the lives of others. That struck her, and then drew her, as a tremendous possibility for the good. Plato put it this way, if you'll forgive his slightly awkward construction. What is love, he asks at one point? Perhaps not so much the desire for beauty, as the desire to give birth in beauty (*Symposium* 206e5): in the beauty of her relationship in my friend's case.

To put it more generally, relationships work best when they focus not on themselves but on that which is beyond them. They are then creative, we might say, a creativity that need not just be to do with offspring. I recall a comment made in a televised interview by the architect Daniel Libeskind. He said that if you want to design buildings that are not just one individual's project, and not just the product of a particular time – but that might echo across all time – you need one thing: to love. He could have been referring solely to his well-known love for his wife or to his obvious love of beautiful things. But he seemed to imply instead that they are particularly precious manifestations of something universal; I sensed that he meant you need to stand in love, be possessed by it, to live the truly creative life – that is to touch transcendence.

Or I recall the love that Margaret Wilcox longs for in E. M. Forster's novel *Howards End*. Her husband, Henry, is too controlled. He is what someone might call "a good man", damning with faint praise. As Margaret sees it, his goodness yields a self-satisfaction that is obtuse and fragmented; it is as dusty prose to the ardent poetry she desires. "Only connect!", she pleads, providing Forster with the opportunity to expound what was virtually a creed:

> ... she might yet be able to help him to the building of the rainbow bridge that should connect the prose in us with the passion. Without it we are meaningless fragments, half monks, half beasts, unconnected arches that have never joined into a man. With it love is born, and alights on the highest curve, glowing against the grey, sober against the fire. Happy the man who sees from either aspect the glory of these outspread wings. (2006: 158)

Astonishing buildings and rainbow bridges are two other kinds of creativity that might emerge in love.

The power of such love is that it speaks so immediately to us of these things. When directed aright it has a capacity like no other to carry us farther. It is drawn by that which is both appealing and good; it gives rise to the transcendent perspective on life by sensitizing the individual to those things that possess the two qualities of beauty and excellence in abundance. The emotional part of ourselves has a physical and spiritual aspect, captured in the wild stud and noble horse, respectively. Or, there is an emotional dynamic within us that is susceptible to reason, as well as the straightforwardly rational part, represented by the noble horse and the charioteer. Or, the completeness of individuality is discovered in the intimacies of relationship, and the one grows out of the other. Love inculcates a wider *joie de vivre* and drives a higher flourishing.

It is also the aching that makes parted hearts grow fonder. It is the desire to realize a goal in a life lest that life be thought deficient for its lack of that goal. In transcendent terms, Eros is also the go-between love: horizontally between human beings; vertically between the world of appearances and the transcendent. He is the *daimon* of *eudaimonia*. Eros wants not so much just more as "the more". He opens eyes to wonder. He mediates mystery. When he does, it feels like pure inspiration; or should that be possession?

Tainted and tough love

This can all sound very fine but it begs a question: if love is good it can also be mad, messy and dangerous. It can turn inwards and become narcissistic. People can say they love one thing, when their actions reveal that really they love something quite different: the politician who speaks of service as he pursues naked power; the wife who speaks of commitment as she conducts her extra-marital affairs. For most people, no doubt, love begins with selfish concerns: the desire to have another, to possess their beauty, to be recognized by them. This is the power of the dark horse. Moreover, the experience of being in love, although glorious, can also feel uncomfortable. Along with the passion it ignites come all kinds of irritations, obsessions and schemes. The lover can also be a plotter, consciously or not aiming to provoke words of affection, to contrive chance meetings, to force a feeling of dependence from his or her beloved.

It can be self-serving in a way that makes it quite repulsive to one at the thick end of its affection. Many disillusioned website authors quote the character Rose Walker in Neil Gaiman's graphic novel *The Kindly Ones*:

Have you ever been in love? ... Horrible isn't it? ... It makes you so vulnerable. It opens your chest and it opens up your heart and it means someone can get inside you and mess you up. You build up all these defenses, you build up a whole suit of armor, so that nothing can hurt you, then one stupid person, no different from any other stupid person, wanders into your stupid life ...

You give them a piece of you. They didn't ask for it. They did something dumb one day, like kiss you or smile at you, and then your life isn't your own anymore.

Love takes hostages. It gets inside you. It eats you out and leaves you crying in the darkness, so simple a phrase like 'maybe we should be just friends' turns into a glass splinter working its way into your heart.

... It hurts. Not just in the imagination. Not just in the mind. *It's a soul-hurt, a real gets-inside-you-and-rips-you-apart pain.*

... I hate love.   (1999)

There is another myth that speaks of this. It tells of love's origins. It turns out that the personified Eros was conceived on the night that Aphrodite was born. There was a party in heaven and there Poros, the god of resourcefulness, son of Metis, the god of cunning, got drunk on nectar, as gods are wont to do. He fell asleep in Zeus' garden, and while he was drowsy, Penia, the god of poverty, aroused him and she became pregnant. Eros was the product of their congress: they literally made Love. But Eros' grandmother, Metis, is the god of cunning. Eros can sometimes be a wily trickster.

So, Eros is the offspring of gods; he is not a god himself. He is imperfect. How could he be otherwise when he longs for what is beautiful and good, something the gods don't do, being directly acquainted with such things. If you want to introduce some more Freud into the discussion, this is to say that love can evoke transference: the lover then projecting all kinds of anxieties and neuroses onto their beloved. Transference is not a step forwards let alone upwards but a step back, a repetition of past behaviour and feeling that aims to keep the world the same and contained, which is to say recognizable to the individual because that is what they've always known. This kind of love is loath to come out of itself. It wants to bolster the barriers of the ego. Transference has its metaphysical counterpart, if I can put it like that, which is wariness of the transcendent: another kind of experience that is unknown. As transference rehearses what it knows, so the refusal of the transcendent becomes an exercise in rejecting possibilities on the grounds that they are troubling to the ego of the human intellect. Thus for some today the love of the transcendent is neurotic; it is neither plausible nor coherent.

Other manifestations of love's potential for ill-being can be sketched by turning back to Plato's metaphor. Consider how the charioteer would be incapacitated if the white horse became lame. He would be severely compromised in terms of driving towards the richer possibilities to be found within love and friendship. He might try to prevent the black horse from simply leaping on its object of desire, that is, try to guide it away from the quick but ambivalent satisfactions of pure pleasure. However, not being able to work the white horse, the main tool he would have at his disposal would be the whip. While the whip might be able to force the black horse to pull in a direction it did not wish to go, the result would be far from the ideal image of wellbeing, a charioteer in harmony with his steeds. In modern psychological terms, the image of the flawed team seems to mirror a hedonistic individual who is an addict; someone caught, say, in a perpetual cycle of sexual thrill followed by post-coital shame, being unable to control the urges that churn within them or to nurture the skills required to hold down a relationship. Or, given a wider definition of lust, such as a lust for money or food, the same image would embrace the greedy personality, on a perpetual search for ever greater financial power or culinary indulgence. It is love as a drug.

Or it is possible to think of ill-being in this way. The white horse is the desire to reach out. In the myth, this culminates in the chariot sprouting wings and developing the ability to fly heavenwards. These are the capacities that open up the individual to higher flourishing. Deny them and, to borrow modern Freudian terms, the individual develops pathologies of self-regard. This is the self-centred life, in which things are pursued for what they deliver, not for what they are in themselves.

Depression could be one result, in the melancholic sense of mourning without knowing quite what that painful loss might be about. Then, as Freud noted, melancholy can lead to violent self-criticism – the whip again – as the individual comes to believe that not only is the world poor, empty and meaningless, but they are themselves too. They may not realize it, but they are missing a part of themselves. The transcendent perhaps? Another manifestation of the crisis we face today over our wellbeing? Alternatively, in the extreme, someone with no capacity to reach beyond themselves becomes a psychopath; or again, someone whose default response is to lash out. Plato suggests as much when at another point he strikingly defines virtue as a "kind of mental health".

After this list of ills, it might seem a small matter to add that ill-being will have no interest in philosophy. This is perhaps a more significant loss than it might first seem when it is noted, as Angie Hobbs has argued in her book *Plato and the Hero*, that Plato developed his concept of the tripartite self and *thumos* partly in response to the challenge of a youthful, thrusting Athenian called Callicles.

The encounter is retold in Plato's dialogue the *Gorgias*. In it, Callicles mocks Socrates for portraying a good life as one in which desires work with reason; Callicles believes that a good life is actually one in which you are able to do as you please, by being, as far as possible, a forceful man of affairs. Callicles has a take on life that Socrates desperately wants to refute, for he believes it undermines a great manifestation of the good in life, namely justice. Callicles' will-to-power approach deforms justice from the question of what is right to a matter of self-interest that favours the strongman. The image of the white horse is part of Socrates' answer, since the implication is that, without it, an individual's will is wild and opportunistic. It is what Callicles lacks. Conversely, the noble or heroic life, one in which the chariot team is on top form, is recognizable precisely because of its love for what is good. Incidentally, in real life Callicles became a tyrant or, to put it another way, a player in the violent politics of the deformed transcendence of totalitarianism.

And yet, for all this risk and taint, for all these ways that crooked love can lead to ill-being, it remains amenable to beauty. Only devilish evil lacks that susceptibility. And beauty is both magnetic and a clue to what is good. Thus, although love may go into a spin like the confused needle of a compass, beneath the local disturbances it will also feel a deeper force, that of the return to true north. To put it another way, there is a kind of shock therapy inherent in love – in the Greek, Plato calls it "backlove", perhaps like a "kickback" – a reaction so strong that it breaks through the defences of the ego and outplays the games of transference. In that moment we see ourselves, and our actions, quite as clearly as if we were looking at ourselves in a mirror. It is love that is humbling because it demands the honesty of knowing yourself. Although, there is a consolation in love too: someone can find that they themselves are loved! It can take them quite by surprise. It can crack the steeliest selfishness, for love comes to us as much as it draws us to others and beyond. Like sun through clouds, the transcendent breaks through.

Much of life, most of the time, is of course characterized by self-concern. Only the saint is egoless. And yet this is only to flag up another side of love that may be profoundly troubling, conscious-changing: "love is the extremely difficult realisation that something other than oneself is real", as Murdoch put it (1999: 215). The thought that love hurts suggests another reflection on the possible meaningfulness of pain too. For to love is to set yourself up to suffer: at the human level, in the stillbirth of foolish infatuation, in the break-up of relationships, in the rejection of children, in bereavement. At times, everything within us can resist these knocks: fear and instinctive self-preservation make people draw back from love's welcome, to echo the words of George Herbert.

There is much about this in Buddhism, too, in the stories in which a disciple asks the master a question, such as "What is Zen?", and the master responds by breaking the disciple's nose, or condemning them to years of menial tasks. It is painful, it offends the ego, but it is not intended to cause harm. It is done in love. The point is that enlightenment requires a new perspective that necessitates a jolt, even a violent jolt, out of old selfishness. And remember, that there is a lot of laughter in Zen, for to laugh at yourself is a delightfully decentring occurrence when it happens.

There is a Zen-like story told about Socrates. One day a dispassionate young man approached the Greek philosopher and casually said, "O great Socrates, I come to you for knowledge." The philosopher took the young man down to the sea, waded in with him, and then dunked him under the water for thirty seconds. When he let the young man up for air, Socrates asked him to repeat what he wanted. "Knowledge, O great one," he spluttered. Socrates put him under the water again, only this time a little longer. After repeated dunkings and responses, the philosopher asked, "What do you want?" The young man finally gasped, "Air. I want air!" "Good," answered Socrates. "Now, when you want knowledge as much as you wanted air, you shall have it."

The encounter could be interpreted in a number of ways. Perhaps Socrates saw the young man's dispassion and wanted to teach him that philosophy – the love of wisdom, the great yearning for something you lack, like the air so painfully desired by the drowning man – can hurt. Perhaps Socrates saw that the young man was not in love with a desire for knowledge but a desire of Socrates, hence all the exhorting, "O great Socrates". That man needed to abandon his attachment for the ancient philosopher and discover a desire for the transcendent. Whatever the interpretation, it seems to be a story about the shock therapy of love. Speak the truth in love, said St Paul, and you can never go too far wrong.

The good and the godly

The way *eros* awakens individuals to the possibility of transcendence draws attention to our "in-between" status as creatures: we are animals, breathing and breeding bodies that eventually die – we have *zoē*. But we are animals with a human nature, which is to say that we are conscious of our passing status and entertain the possibility that we might glimpse, even partake, in that which is not passing, if only to a degree. This self-awareness makes for the difference between us and our evolutionary cousins. It is why people ask why there is something not nothing. From it springs the distinctively human faculty for creativity that lies at the origins of culture, science, art and language. It is *bios*.

The insight is instructive in another way too, for the self-knowledge it can bring is the source of human wisdom. Socrates put it this way: it was not that he knew much about himself or the world around, as only the gods do, but that he understood how little he knew. He regarded himself as ignorant, although not in the way that animals are, entirely indifferent to their state, but as prudent human beings can be, namely, conscious of the fact. A little knowledge is a dangerous thing and so Socratic wisdom is striving to appreciate where human limitations lie. Hence the constant presence of mystery.

As we also said before, though, this is not a counsel of despair, as if all attempts at knowledge should therefore be abandoned. Quite the opposite. For we are not just self-aware creatures but self-aware creatures who love. This desire for what we lack, supremely so in the case of the transcendent, powers the drive to reach out. It is precisely this dimension of the human condition that allows us to love, that makes us lovers. And it is love that makes for wellbeing. In *The Greeks and Greek Love*, James Davidson breaks this experience of being "in-between" lovers down into two moments. First, there is the desire to "shrink distances": horizontally and humanly, the distance between yourself and the one you love; vertically and tran-scendently, the distance between yourself and meaningful mystery. Secondly, there is the capacity to "make leaps": leaps of love, one might say. These are characterized not just by their passion but by the fact that they cannot be guaranteed a safe landing on the other side. To take such a leap is to step into the unknown. In making a leap we move, as lovers do, beyond the rational. It might throw you seriously out of balance! "The stress is on seeking truth, not on finding it, on pursuing, not on catching", Davidson writes (2007: 216): another reflection of humankind's "in-between" nature. We know we lack, but are never quite sure what we lack. And we know that to be human we must constantly reach out for all that we will never entirely pin down. What saves us from being the most ridicu-lous of creatures, though, is that this loving transforms our exist-ence from one of just living, to one of living fully. It injects the spirited and the spiritual. It is our wellbeing.

To put it another way, our "in-between" nature allows us to look up, as befits the intelligent animal who walks on two legs not four. Thus it is that religion is an almost universal human activity. Plato himself did not have the word "religion". He did put the desire for what is good – the religious spirit – at the heart of his account of wellbeing. Perhaps it is often difficult to distinguish between the search for the good and the search for God. It was natural for the early Christians, in their borrowing from Platonic thought, to take up his analysis of the human predicament and interpret it from within their explicitly theistic frame. Augustine, for one, referred to the state of being "in-between" too, if rather more poetically when he said that we are "between beasts and angels". Similarly, if love moves in between divine wisdom and terrestrial ignorance, then the love of what is good and the love of God might easily coincide because God is good.

They do for people of faith, in the sense that they have a belief in a personal God; they don't in exclusive humanism. But what of the middle way that I've been pursuing here, that of the religiously inclined agnostic? What might this movement of love say to them about the nature of things?

Philosophically, the question is often put this way: is something good because some god has decreed it, or is it good by virtue of some property it has in itself? The former option is problematic to the humanist imagination since it appears to make goodness arbitrary, as if the same god might one day change its mind about what is good and thus the definition of goodness. Many contemporary philosophers, atheistic and religious, would prefer to say that goodness is self-defining. This makes sense because we do have partial intuitions about what goodness is, for all that, of course, people also disagree. Although, as Wittgenstein remarked, if you write God out of the equation, you imply that such important matters rest in human hands, which is hardly grounds for confidence.

And yet, is that exactly right? For the question of the good is not just a matter of definition, because the moral life at heart is not just about asking whether this or that is good, or even trying to do good. It is about actually becoming good in the sense of embodying something of the good in life. The religious conception of wellbeing defines the goal as understanding the good: understanding in the intimate sense of "I know that feeling" not just "I know that tune". To put it another way, we love goodness because it is something that draws us: at its root, love is something that happens to us; we can work on becoming more loving only by responding to love. For the rightly attuned person, goodness has an irresistible allure. This implies something else: love lies at the heart of the moral life – the complex longing for what is good mixed in with the consciousness of always lacking it, always being somewhat confused about it. In this understanding of ethics, it is not ultimately the consequences of actions, or the duty to perform them, or even a sympathy for our fellows that makes us moral: all qualities on which subsequent philosophers have hung their moral theories. They matter and are important because, with the best will in the world, human beings are flawed: a call of duty, an obligation to another or a decision based on a calculation will help everyone, sometimes, to act more morally. That is just to be realistic. But the primary concern, if the goal is wellbeing – life improved from the inside out – is what you love. "Love and do what you will", Augustine wrote, catching the non-utilitarian nature of love. Plato would have agreed. It is a vision of the good in life, of wellbeing, that doesn't depend first on believing in God or, as the secular individual might put it, on first answering the question "What is good?", for that is never quite clear. Instead, it rests on love.

To put it another way, the moral life might be defined as a stirring and training of the attention, prompted by love, that reorientates the way someone looks at the world towards the good. Unsettled by its energy, it is a struggle against egoism and an awakening of compassion. This is more than just a refining of habits and customs, as Hume tells us, although no doubt the habits and customs of an individual will become more like assets than vices in a life that is lived well. It is a spiritual change, spiritual in the sense of becoming alert to more than the business that shapes the everyday. "The good life becomes increasingly selfless through an increased awareness of, sensibility to, the world beyond the self", says Murdoch (1992: 53). As long as the lover holds on to the beauty that first drew them, virtues will be stirred – alongside some vices, particularly in the early days – because love is desire for the good, and wellbeing is living alongside the good. There is a synthesis here, reflected in the Greek word for beauty, *kalos*, which also means good and honourable, and, as an adverb, rightly and happily!

The link between what we now call religion and morality – or God and the good – comes to look very different when love is viewed as the midwife of the good in life, as the force that delivers wellbeing to us. There are "religious modes of thought deep inside morals", says Murdoch (*ibid*.: 304). For if to be moral is more than just to reason about what is good and then to attempt to do it, but is to cultivate a good life that shows through the good in life, then understanding what is good is linked to our capacity for it. Knowledge is close to being; practice opens up new horizons. That intimacy with the good can be steered by reason but more profoundly develops, or not, according to the way we live, day by day, hour by hour, minute by minute. Practical intelligence matters more than theoretical intelligence. As Nietzsche inferred, we become what we are. A good life, then, is close to a spiritual exercise. It feels like taking a long pilgrimage towards a holy place or an attempt to be so changed that it becomes possible to catch a glimpse of perfection. Here we are remaining uncommitted about the existence of any deity. It is easy to see, though, how such directed movement might well be imagined as coming close to holiness. If the meek are blessed, then blessed also are the pure in heart, "for they shall see God".

The ascent

It is also easy to see how this vision of wellbeing links back to spiritual experience. For love is like a ladder. On the lower rungs is manifest a passionate attraction for a particular individual. Like the story in the *Phaedrus*, this does not just please the body but warms the heart, affording the lovers not just a delight in each other but a deeper appreciation of the joys of life in general. Friendship stirs a higher thirst. They climb further and, as they do, become aware not just of the splendour of physical beauty but the beauty inherent in, say, the insights of science or understanding gained through the arts. This is an aesthetic appreciation of what human capacities can grasp of the world around them. It generates a sense of wonder: wonder at the limits of human knowledge, too, perceived more clearly by the increase in knowledge. The fired imagination drives them higher again as magnificent abstract truths come to appeal to them. We might envisage here an awareness of reality that is able to grasp the unchanging simplicity of things in themselves through the miasma of change and multiplicity that otherwise fills and obscures life: it is to gasp at existence – being – in itself; it is to be well-practised at mindfulness. Then, finally, at the pinnacle of the ascent, the "goal of loving", that which is "wonderfully beautiful in its nature", is seen. It opens the "eye of the soul" to that which is good in itself. This step is as different from the previous one as having a glorious vista described for you and then seeing it for yourself. Or it is like the moment when instead of having to translate the words of a foreign language into your native tongue you instinctively comprehend what is being said. You have developed a fluency and an intimacy with what you love. Virtue is implicitly understood. Like a religious experience, for a moment at least, your consciousness of being alive is transformed. You've been with the good in life.

This is the mystical experience that Plato describes at the climax of the *Symposium*. It is a dynamic that grounds meaning through three levels of transcendence: the embodied, the intellectual and the spiritual. They all share in the good but according to this understanding the one must lead to the other for the fullness of wellbeing to be known. It begins with lower flourishing, and for those who do

not discard the possibility that this can be a window to an appreciation of things that is beyond straightforward human articulacy, can
lead to mysterious and mystical intuitions of the transcendent.

So is all now forever clear? Will the individual at the top of this
ascent become detached from worldly concerns and sail off into the
Elysium sunset? Well no, not quite. For one thing, they will have a
concern for others: the lover with whom they first found the ladder,
and more widely with others – they are the friends who joyfully
exclaim, "Do you see the same truth?!" Or, like Plato himself, they
will want to spread the word: communicate philosophy, strange as
that may seem. It is not going too far to relate this sense of awakened
care for others with that of the Buddha, who, on gaining enlightenment, embarked on his compassion offensive. They have a more
intense sense of what might lie above and can show some of that
transcendence to others. More profoundly, even the enlightened
are still limited creatures. They have known more but will spend a
lifetime digesting the significance of what that means, for all that
they know it means much. They must wrestle with doubts even
as they glimpse mystery's radiance, for, like a god, it is known as
unknown. Wellbeing for us is also always about living with uncertainties. It is hopeful agnosticism.

Plato himself recognizes this, to my mind, in the following
way. In the *Symposium*, he describes the beatific vision as something that happens "all of a sudden". The Greek is *exaiphanēs*.
The word is important, for the last thing that occurs is not that
Socrates and those with whom he has been discussing this beatific
vision fall into silent, rapt contemplation, as might be expected
following so profound a revelation. Rather, they are rudely interrupted by a drunken, boisterous and renowned beauty of a man
called Alcibiades, who bursts into the room where they have been
conversing, surrounded by dancing girls and flute-players. He is a
sometime follower of Socrates, perhaps a former lover. He is also
someone who has lost control of his white horse. He is not subject

to reason but driven by the dark horse and all too ready to leap on any object of his lust.

That, as they say, is another story. Now, though, observe how Plato describes this riotous entrance. Alcibiades too appears "all of a sudden", *exaiphanēs* (*Symposium* 212c). It is as if his fine looks were a rival to the beauty of the transcendent good. It is as if Plato is acknowledging that things, even the transcendent, can always be interpreted in multiple ways, perceived in a different light. Such is the in-between nature of the human condition. We have a sense of what is good, but maybe only negatively – apophatically – in the sense that we long for something we don't have, or barely conceive, perhaps because we have mostly experienced what is its opposite, the not so good. Or perhaps the transcendent is a kind of superstition, an evolutionarily by-product, or just a poetic expression of the mundane desire to be good and live a life of satisfying-enough projects that maybe somehow make sense altogether. With the appearance of Alcibiades, this man of misaligned affections and obvious vices, it is as if Plato is holding his hands up. He is hanging a question mark over the whole experience. But as was the case with the in-between condition, which Socrates pointed out actually makes love possible, this uncertainty is not bad *per se*. We can try to be good, can attempt the climb – to place that aspiration at the heart of our way of life – for all that the peak is shrouded in cloud so that even on a good day the mists lift only a little. That needn't thwart our love of it.

In her imitation of a platonic dialogue, *Acastos*, Murdoch puts some words into the mouth of Socrates that are relevant. She has Socrates say to Plato:

Man is not the measure of things, we don't just invent our values, we live by a higher law, yet we can't fully explain how this is so. Everything is in a way less deep and in a way deeper than you think. You want a long explanation, but in the end

your explanation repeats what you knew at the start ... If we
do good things which are near to us we may improve a little
... Goodness is simple, it's just very difficult.   (1999: 525)

A way of life

Plato and Socrates could have been lovers too. We know that they
were intimates: Plato only mentions himself three times in his
dialogues, on all three occasions at Socrates' deathbed, where he
lists himself among other close friends. We can be confident that
meeting Socrates was the turning point in his life. He was only
twenty-eight when Socrates died in 399 BCE, and for the remaining
fifty years of his life he dedicated himself to the discovery and articulation of a way of life that he called philosophy in order to make
sense of this unforgettable encounter. It was too good to forget;
perhaps too good to be true. Indeed, there is evidence to think
that Plato came to think of meeting Socrates as a kind of religious
experience in itself, perhaps like coming close to a living saint. At
another point in the *Symposium*, Plato paints a picture of Socrates
as a figure of divine poverty, not unlike the iconography of saint-
hood that exists to this day if you think of individuals such as the
Dalai Lama or Mother Theresa. The point about saints is not that
they are perfect: they have flaws; they are human. Rather, it is that
they are remarkable instantiations of wellbeing, being close to the
good and so mediating, even radiating, transcendence. They have
what might be called spiritual charisma. It is the kind of inspiration that does not just leave people feeling good, as if they had
shaken the hand of a celebrity, but prompts them – empowers them
– to change their lives for the good. In fact, meeting a saint might
not feel good at all, but more like a crisis. "Love is the extremely
difficult realisation that something other than oneself is real". Plato
records individuals having such reactions on meeting Socrates. The

experience caused them to entirely re-evaluate their lives in ways that were very difficult, more akin to suffering than pleasure.

The suggestion is that Socrates was one of the enlightened few who has made the ascent and received the vision, and then returned to help people like Plato. In other words, Socrates was responsible for Plato's conversion. It was he that helped him see through the shadows and brave the sun. Socrates opened Plato's "eye of the soul" on to the transcendent.

Could he do the same for us too? Is he, as Murdoch used to say, a man for our times once more? "In the strange cosmic astronomy of the wandering zeitgeist we are closer to Plato now than in many previous centuries", she wrote (1999: 175). The philosopher Julia Annas makes the helpful suggestion that Plato's understanding of enlightenment is not one that brings certainty, as if suddenly all questioning ceases. Rather, it brings clarity as to the point of it all, that is, the good as a focus for the fundamentals of human well-being. It informs mundane life rather than being a divine trans-portation of the individual away from it. It brings innate meaning not completion; it shows good ends not brings to an end; it enables someone to say that life makes sense and be confident that they can lead their life aright – if they are prepared to put in the effort. For they must still live it. That is partly a cognitive task, although as the myth of the two-horse chariot makes clear, reason is only one faculty to deploy in pursuit of higher flourishing. (If enlightenment was just a question of being analytically capable, all rational people would be Platonists, which they are not, and no rational people would suffer the existential crisis of meaninglessness, which many do.) As another contemporary philosopher, Anthony Price, has put it: "Love may be the best helper not because it provides reasons, but because, in a promising soul well prompted, it is receptive of, and responsive to, the opening of new vistas" (1997: 42). For love is recognition: "re-cognition", Plato said, for the experience feels more like the remembrance of something you already knew, deep down.

To live well is to construct a way of life that cultivates that sight. Theoretical wisdom is a guide but it is the practical wisdom of, well, practice that enlightens.

Perhaps this can be Plato's suggestion to us too. He does not conceive of this moment as a departure from the world, as if it were an assumption into heaven. Like the Buddhist masters, Plato's vision enlivens the world not negates it, uses the body not deprecates it. To live was always to live, body and soul: love is a holistic education. He believed that philosophy was an exercise in learning how to die, but only because that is the best way to learn what you truly love. It brings focus, forces the attention. Enlightenment changes everything but it is also marked by a new searching as the individual tries to work it out. Nothing is conclusively solved: everything is continually addressed afresh. That doesn't just take a lifetime, it takes a life, and a life lived well at that. Perhaps Plato's attempts at capturing it in his writing are his coming to terms with a religious experience that he never quite unpacks. He never would; how could he? Instead, he was always seeking new angles on it, approaching the truth of it circuitously, at a slant.

We must do the same. The good is simple, it is just very difficult. What can be secured, though, is a taste for the mystery of things, of transcendence that is as unputdownable as it is indescribable as it is illuminating. We love beauty; we are drawn to the good. It is a vision of life beyond happiness and pleasure, rules and duty, even meaning and virtue – although they are all part of it. By seeking the good in life you find wellbeing.

Forster, E. M. 2006. *Howards End*. Harmondsworth: Penguin.

Frankl, V. E. 1959. *Man's Search for Meaning*. Boston, MA: Beacon.

Freud, S. [1895] 2004. "On the Pscyhotherapy of Hysteria". In Sigmund Freud & J. Breuer, *Studies in Hysteria*, N. Luckhurst (trans.), 255–306. Harmondsworth: Penguin.

Fromm, E. 1956. *The Art of Loving*. New York: Harper Perennial.

Gaiman, M. 1999. *The Sandman 9: The Kindly Ones*. New York: DC Comics.

Haidt, J. 2003. "Elevation and the Positive Psychology of Morality", unedited manuscript, http://faculty.virginia.edu/haidtlab/articles/haidt.elevation-and-positive-psychology.manuscript.html (accessed April 2008). Later published in *Flourishing: Positive Psychology and the Life Well-lived*, C. L. M. Keyes & J. Haidt (eds), 275–89. Washington DC: American Psychological Association.

Haidt, J. 2006. *The Happiness Hypothesis: Putting Ancient Wisdom and Philosophy to the Test of Modern Science*. London: Arrow.

Heidegger, M. 1972. *What is Called Thinking*, J. G. Gray & F. D. Wieck (trans.). New York: Harper & Row.

Hick, J. 2006. *The New Frontier of Religion and Science: Religious Experience, Neuroscience and the Transcendent*. Basingstoke: Palgrave Macmillan.

Hobbs, A. 2000. *Plato and the Hero: Courage, Manliness and the Impersonal Good*. Cambridge: Cambridge University Press.

Hofstadter, D. 1980. "Reductionism and Religion". *Behavioural and Brain Sciences* **3**: 433–4.

Hume, D. 1960. *A Treatise of Human Nature*. Oxford: Oxford University Press.

Huxley, A, 2004a. *The Perennial Philosophy*. New York: Harper Perennial.

Huxley, A. 2004b. *Brave New World*. London: Vintage.

James, O. 2008. *The Selfish Capitalist*. London: Vermilion.

James, W. 1982. *The Varieties of Religious Experience*. Harmondsworth: Penguin.

Jaspers, K. 2003. *Way To Wisdom: An Introduction to Philosophy*. New Haven, CT: Yale University Press.

Kandinsky, W. 1977. *Concerning the Spiritual in Art*. New York: Dover.

Kerr, F. 1997. *Immortal Longings: Versions of Transcending Humanity*. London: SPCK.

Kierkegaard, S. 1978. *Parables of Kierkegaard*, Thomas C. Oden (ed.). Princeton, NJ: Princeton University Press.

Layard, R. 2007. *Happiness: Lessons for a New Science*. Harmondsworth: Penguin.

Leader, D. 2008. *The New Black: Mourning, Melancholia and Depression*. London: Hamish Hamilton.

Lear, G. R. 2004. *Happy Lives and the Highest Good: An Essay on Aristotle's Nicomachean Ethics*. Princeton, NJ: Princeton University Press.

Lewis, C. S. 1960. *The Four Loves*. London: Collins.

Marar, Z. 2003. *The Happiness Paradox*. London: Reaktion.

McCabe, H. 2005. *The Good Life*. London: Continuum.

Mill, J. S. 1989. *Autobiography*. Hardmondsworth: Penguin.

Further reading

Ever since Plato, the subject of happiness has prompted many authors to put pen to paper, and not least in the past ten years, since Martin Seligman, as President of the American Psychological Association, championed the study of positive psychology. When I've referred to popular advice on happiness, it is mostly this work – otherwise referred to as the new science of happiness – that I have in mind. The key texts with which I have either explicitly or implicitly engaged are: Martin Seligman's *Authentic Happiness: Using the New Positive Psychology to Realize Your Potential for Lasting Fullfilment* (2003); Richard Layard's *Happiness: Lessons from a New Science* (2005); Tal Ben-Shahar's *Happier* (2007) and Jonathan Haidt's *The Happiness Hypothesis: Putting Ancient Wisdom and Philosophy to the Test of Modern Science* (2006) – the last being the most in sympathy with the approach I've taken here.

For an alternative examination of why there appears to be a crisis about happiness in the modern world, try Oliver James' *The Selfish Capitalist* (2008). And for a personal and accessible discussion of neuroscience, happiness and consciousness see Jeff Warren's *Head Trip: Adventures on the Wheel of Consciousness* (2007). To unpack the religious and philosophical implications of these sciences, John Hick's *The New Frontier of Religion and Science: Religious Experience, Neuroscience and the Transcendent* (2006) is careful and succinct.

Aristotle is a good place to start when engaging with the ancient philosophers. Two of his works on *eudaimonia* have come down to us, the *Eudemian Ethics* and the *Nicomachean Ethics*. They exist in various translations in English and have produced a voluminous secondary literature. One of the most recent and best is Gabriel Richardson Lear's *Happy Lives and the Highest Good: An Essay on Aristotle's Nicomachean Ethics* (2004).

When it comes to Plato, his dialogues the *Phaedrus* and the *Symposium* combine immediate readability with rewarding detailed study. Good translations are those by Nehamas and Woodruff, published by Hackett. They also provide excellent introductions. For Iris Murdoch's take on Plato, her *Metaphysics as a Guide to Morals* (1992) is indispensable. All her other relevant non-fiction works have been usefully collected by Peter Conradi in *Existentialists and Mystics: Writings on Philosophy and Literature* (1999).

The broad shape of the history of ideas since the Renaissance, and particularly the notions of higher and lower flourishing, I have taken from Charles Taylor's *A*

Secular Age (2007). It is a long book and gathers an extraordinary amount of material, is remarkably even-handed, and sparkles with insights.

For introductions to Buddhist thought by someone with a keen interest in Western philosophy see Jean-François Revel and Matthieu Ricard, *The Monk and the Philosopher* (1998); and for the same by someone with a keen interest in Western psychology see Matthieu Ricard *Happiness: A Guide to Developing Life's Most Important Skills* (2003).

When it comes to the overlap between ancient philosophy, psychology and religion, try John Cottingham, *The Spiritual Dimension: Religion, Philosophy and Human Value* (2005). And for notions of transcendence implicit in many contemporary philosophers, not least Iris Murdoch, see Fergus Kerr, *Immortal Longings: Versions of Transcending Humanity* (1997).

References

Annas, J. 1981. *An Introduction to Plato's Republic*. Oxford: Clarendon Press.

Aristotle. 2002. *Nicomachean Ethics*. Oxford: Oxford University Press.

Aristotle. 1992. *Eudemian Ethics*. Oxford: Clarendon Press.

Armstrong, K. 2000. *Buddha*. London: Phoenix.

Aurelius, M. 2006. *Meditations*. Harmondsworth: Penguin.

Ben-Shahar, T. 2007. *Happier: Finding Pleasure, Meaning and Life's Ultimate Currency*. London: McGraw-Hill.

Bentham, J. 1996. *An Introduction to the Principles of Morals and Legislation*. Oxford: Clarendon Press.

Carrette, J. & R. King 2005. *Selling Spirituality: The Silent Takeover of Religion*. London: Routledge.

Conradi, P. 1999. *Existentialists and Mystics: Writings on Philosophy and Literature*. Harmondsworth: Penguin.

Cooper, D. E. 2003. *Meaning*. Chesham: Acumen.

Cottingham, J. 2005. *The Spiritual Dimension: Religion, Philosophy and Human Value*. Cambridge: Cambridge University Press.

Dalai Lama & Howard C. Cutler 1998. *The Art of Happiness: A Handbook for Living*. Philadelphia, PA: Coronet.

Darwin, C. 1981. *The Descent of Man, and Selection in Relation to Race*. Princeton, NJ: Princeton University Press.

Davidson, J. 2007. *The Greeks and Greek Love: A Radical Reappraisal of Homosexuality in Ancient Greece*. London: Weidenfeld & Nicolson.

Davies, B. 1993. *The Thought of Thomas Aquinas*. Oxford: Clarendon Press.

Davies, P. 2006. *The Goldilocks Enigma*. London: Allen Lane.

Durkheim, E. 1970. *Suicide*. London: Routledge & Kegan Paul.

Ehrenreich, B. 2007 *Dancing in the Streets: A History of Collective Joy*. London: Granta.

Emerson, R. W. 1841. "Love". www.rwe.org/works/Essays-1st_Series_05_Love.htm (accessed April 2008).

Epicurus 1994. *The Epicurus Reader*, B. Inwood & L. P. Gerson (ed. and trans.). Indianapolis, IN: Hackett.

Flew, A. 2000. "Tolstoi and the Meaning of Life". In *The Meaning of Life*, E. D. Klemke (ed.), 209–18. Oxford: Oxford University Press.

Montefiore, H. 1995. *Oh God, What Next?* London: Hodder & Stoughton.

Murdoch, I. 1958. *The Bell*. London: Chatto & Windus.

Murdoch, I. 1992. *Metaphysics as a Guide to Morals*. Harmondsworth: Penguin.

Murdoch, I. 1999. *Existentialists and Mystics: Writings on Philosophy and Literature*, Peter Conradi (ed.). Harmondsworth: Penguin.

Nabokov, V. 1969. Conversation with James Mossman. *The Listener*, 23 October.

Nietzsche, F. 1974. *The Gay Science*. New York: Vintage.

Nozick, R. 1974. *Anarchy, State and Utopia*. New York: Basic Books.

Orwell, G. 1945. "Notes on Nationalism". www.george-orwell.org/Notes_on_Nationalism/0.html (accessed April 2008).

Pirsig, R. M. 1974. *Zen and the Art of Motorcycle Maintenance*. London: Corgi.

Plato 1995. *Phaedrus*, Alexander Nehamas & Paul Woodruff (trans.). Indianapolis, IN: Hackett.

Plato 1989. *Symposium*, Alexander Nehamas & Paul Woodruff (trans.). Indianapolis, IN: Hackett.

Popper, K. 2002. *Unended Quest*. London: Routledge.

Price, A. 1997. *Love and Friendship in Plato and Aristotle*. Oxford: Clarendon Press.

Revel, J.-F. & M. Ricard 1998. *The Monk and the Philosopher*. London: Schocken Books.

Ricard, M. 2003. *Happiness: A Guide to Developing Life's Most Important Skills* London: Atlantic.

Russell, B. 1903. "A Free Man's Worship". http://users.drew.edu/~jlenz/fmw.html (accessed April 2008).

Russell, B. 1997. *Religion and Science*. Oxford: Oxford University Press.

Schleiermacher, F. 1988. *On Religion: Speeches to its Cultured Despisers* Cambridge: Cambridge University Press.

Seligman. M. 2003. *Authentic Happiness: Using the New Positive Psychology to Realize Your Potential for Lasting Fulfilment*. London: Nicholas Brealey.

Seligman, M. 2007. "The First Coming". www.edge.org/q2007/q07_3.html (accessed April 2008).

Singer, P. 1997. *How are We to Live?* Oxford: Oxford University Press.

Steiner, G. 1989. *Real Presences*. Chicago, IL: University of Chicago Press.

Tallis, R. 2007. *The Enduring Significance of Parmenides: Unthinkable Thought*. London: Continuum.

Tallis, R. 2008. "Parmenides". *Prospect* **142** (January). www.prospect-magazine. co.uk/article_details.php?id=9972 (accessed April 2008).

Taylor, C. 2007. *A Secular Age*. Cambridge, MA: Harvard University Press.

Tolstoy, L. 1987. *A Confession and Other Religious Writings*. Harmondsworth: Penguin.

Traherne, T. 2002. *Centuries of Meditations*. In *Thomas Traherne: Poetry and Prose*, Denise Inge (ed.). London: SPCK.

Trilling, L. 1972. *Sincerity and Authenticity*. Cambridge, MA: Harvard University Press.

Wallas, G. 1999. *The Art of Thought*. London: Vintage.

Warren, J. 2007. *Head Trip: Adventures on the Wheel of Consciousness*. Oxford: Oneworld.

Watts, A. 1999. *The Way of Zen*. London: Vintage.

Williams, R. 2003. *Lost Icons*. London: Continuum.

Wittgenstein, L. 1981. *Notebooks*. Oxford: Blackwell.

Wright, R. 2000. *Nonzero*. London: Abacus.

Index